CRITICAL THINKING

A Guide to Interpreting Literary Texts

CRITICAL THINKING
A Guide to Interpreting Literary Texts

Colin Manlove

Reader in English Literature
University of Edinburgh

St. Martin's Press   New York

First published in the United States of America of 1989

Printed in Hong Kong

ISBN 0–312–03166–1

Library of Congress Cataloging-in-Publication Data
Manlove, C. N. Colin Nicholas, 1942–
Critical thinking: a guide to interpreting literary texts/
    Colin Manlove
        p.   cm.
    Bibliography: p.
    Includes index
    ISBN 0–312–03166–1
    1. English literature – History and criticism – Theory, etc.
2. Critical thinking.   3. Criticism.   I. Title.
PR21.M28   1989
801'95–dc19   89–30824
                                                        CIP

10   9   8   7   6   5   4   3   2

Contents

Thought is free.
The Tempest

Where the reader is referred to as 'he', 'he' or 'she' is implied.

For Evelyn

Acknowledgements

The author and publishers wish to thank the following who have kindly given permission for the use of copyright material:

Norman MacCaig and Chatto and Windus for 'Explorer' from *A Round of Applause*, and David Higham Associates Ltd for 'And Death Shall Have No Dominion' by Dylan Thomas in *The Poems* (Dent), and New Directions Publishing Corporation for the same poem in *The Poems of Dylan Thomas*, © 1943.

1
Introduction

The object of this book is to suggest some ways of thinking about literature to make it come more alive for the reader. There is nothing more tempting to the critical mind, faced by the seemingly opaque fact of the text, than to slide off into conventional judgements, generalities, historical background or the views of other commentators. The rigour of thought, the long hours, especially for novices, of often unproductive attempts at analysis, are always enormously daunting. There is the feeling that the text will yield so much and no more, that any attempt to go further will only produce wire-drawn interpretations. Surely, after all, one's business is only to add a modest observation or two to the pile of accepted views? But so to submit to the opinions of others is to lose the freedom and individuality of one's own sensibility and the life of the work. And often in any case there are no critics on a given work, or they do not look at it in a way that can be at all absorbed, or ask the sort of questions that occur to the reader. In the end the reader must face the work alone, if his or her ideas are to have any penetration and vitality. And it is that situation to which this book is directed.

The process that now has to go on is one that many critics follow but is not often overtly discussed or described. There are handbooks on how to approach the work of literature by considering themes and stylistic devices, but little that tells the reader how to go about forming ideas in the first place. To some extent, of course, thinking cannot be taught: it is also a matter of practice and instinct. The reader must teach himself to construct a convincing argument: he must teach himself to muster evidence to demonstrate his case without distortion. But there would be no arguments at all without an initial insight into a text that sets the mind moving along lines that open up the whole work. This book sets out to provide some intellectual starting-handles, and to show what can happen when they are used.

But what does this 'thinking' mean? Put like this it may sound rather abstract and divorced from the work. Yet its effect is precisely to put the reader in nearer relation to the text, to encourage him or her to work more closely with the evidence, so closely indeed that the relation between his mind and the text might be described as interpenetration rather than mere observation. Thinking thus, the reader enters into the work, feels its movements, harmonies, jars and jolts. It is a living process and a mobile one. To that extent it is best taught through description more than prescription. And the conclusions arrived at should never be fixed, only tentative, not merely because of each reader's subjectivity but because the experience of the work is a dynamic and mobile one, not static and fixed: the reader will have lived through it as the work has 'lived through' the life it partially imitates, and if anyone ever reads what he says about it they will better understand it by being made to experience the process by which his ideas formed, swung, grouped and coalesced. Ironically, such criticism will if successful be the very kind to take over the minds of its readers – but the effect will be more to excite them to their own explorations than to give them the impression that all is intellectual *terra cognita*. It is for this reason that as well as suggesting ways of opening up literature, this book will try to recreate the excitement with which the connections are first seen. *Try*, only: it is hard to recapture the special luminosity of the ideas when they first occur and when the mind seems suddenly able to jump from point to point of the work until it is almost as though the whole thing turned in one's hands and threw out light from its centre.

The purpose here will thus be in a sense to pull the mind back as much as to suggest means by which it may go further forward – to pull it back to the point where it first succeeds in opening up a text, before the ideas harden into a dead and fixed interpretation. It is an attempt to return to the spontaneity of 'first draft' thinking. To that extent this is an amateur's book: it is written out of a distrust for the professional criticism of literature.

One result of this approach is that many of the readings of

texts are at least partly novel. They do not provide the sorts of received interpretations that form the canon of current critical opinion. It can fairly be claimed that anyone practised in some of the methods to be outlined here will also produce his or her own novel interpretations of works. By 'novel' is not meant 'eccentric' but rather that which, giving the work and the critical mind a new independence one from another, enables features that were unseen or forgotten before to become visible. No guarantee is possible that such readings will become academically accepted, despite the degree to which they can be 'proved'. But what matters is that the critical activity is carried on with both a sober concern for truth backed by evidence, and the kind of pleasure in finding it, that together give back to literature its living and many-faceted character.

The writers and texts discussed are most of them among those that form the staple of any course in English literature. Some receive more attention than others: but in a book where each is an illustration only, this should not affect the issue. The book is addressed primarily to students, whose minds are most elastic and original, if they are often too respectful or lazy to start using them: may they have as much pleasure from books as this writer has often had from discussing them with them.

2
Getting Critical

The first rule is, *never take things for granted*. Our own minds must always be brought into play: we must appropriate the work for ourselves and react freely to it.

As an example, consider this soliloquy by Prince Hal in Shakespeare's *Henry IV Part One*. Hal has been apparently forsaking his royal duties and mixing with a group of tavern dwellers centred on the gross and comical Sir John Falstaff, and we have just been introduced to him in their company. After they have left, Hal turns aside to utter a soliloquy concerning his true stance and intentions regarding Falstaff and his crew:

> I know you all, and will awhile uphold
> The unyok'd humour of your idleness;
> Yet herein will I imitate the sun,
> Who doth permit the base contagious clouds
> To smother up his beauty from the world,
> That, when he please again to be himself,
> Being wanted, he may be more wond'red at
> By breaking through the foul and ugly mists
> Of vapours that did seem to strangle him.
>   (I,ii,188–96)

If we take this at face value, Hal is simply saying that like the sun with clouds, he will allow his time with Falstaff to cover up his true nature from the world so that it will be all the more glorious when eventually revealed. There is nothing particularly questionable in our sense about the idea. But if we think about the image of the sun with which it is conveyed, letting its full character and implications play through our minds, we may begin to see something else. It is a hard process, and it may be a long time before anything gives, by which time we may well have given up and moved on. Prompting us to yield is always the feeling that what is not immediately felt is not there. But 'what is felt' is often hard to isolate. If we discover more in the image, we may feel that it fits with slight sensations we had before but ignored for what seemed the main effect. For instance the tone seems rather cocky, 'I know you all', 'Yet herein will I', 'when he please again', and this may fit with any weakness we find. What of the analogy then? Certainly clouds can cover the sun and then reveal it once more, and this is a good likeness for what Hal thinks he is doing. He is to be the sun, letting this happen. But *do* suns let anything happen? Is it not rather the case that things just happen? Sometimes clouds come and cover the sun; sometimes they pass: that is all. The sun cannot choose when the clouds should come, nor when they should go. But we see that of course Hal has to say this to fit in with his own position: he chooses when to be 'covered' by the cloud of Falstaff, and when not.

We can leave it at that, if we like, with a rather ill-suited image, and say no more. But equally we can do otherwise and ask how it was that he came to use such an image, leaving aside the issue of poor choice. And if we do that, thinking about his position in the rest of the play, quite another idea can develop. The issue already raised by Hal's father, King Henry IV, in the first scene of the play, is how far in quitting the court Hal is being a waster: his father partly thinks so. Here Hal is claiming the opposite, that he is mixing with Falstaff for political reasons. Who is right? We may well feel that Hal's argument is a little specious and wire-drawn before we even consider the analogy. Is it necessary to dirty oneself in order the better to gain people's good opinions? Hal's brothers Prince John and Thomas Duke of Clarence seem at least to have their father's good opinion. Certainly the 'reformation' Hal eventually makes when he becomes king is wondered at, seems even miraculous to those about him, but does this make his kingship more stable? Is it egotism, political skill or altruism that directs him?

Looking again at the sun image, we can see that Hal has to say that he as sun controls the movement of the clouds, because he is claiming that he is in control of his experiences with Falstaff. The meteorological facts are that clouds cover the sun at random. If we play this fact against Hal's assertion, we can see that he is simply not allowing for this reality. Even if we allow, as the Renaissance might have, a measure of free choice or personality to heavenly bodies, there is still this equally valid empirical view. And if this is so, then we feel the second fact to work against the first. Because Hal's analogy does not fully work, so his argument does not quite convince. He may see himself as choosing what he does, and keeping himself in fastidious detachment from Falstaff, but it may equally be that he is more involved with Falstaff than he cares to admit: still more, on this evidence, he himself does not know which it is, does not fully know his own motives or even what he is. And at this point the significance here of the word 'contagious' used of the clouds may well strike us: here, even while he asserts the separation of the sun from the clouds, and the sun's power over them, Hal is admitting their potential contagious influence on him as sun. The word was not called for: it seems thrown in by some subconscious prompting, perhaps based on Hal's repressed sense that he is partly subject to Falstaff.

There is much more to explore in the rest of the soliloquy, where Hal uses another suspect analogy and the questionable argument that to appear to offend will make his eventual reformation more striking. But once we have become alert thus to part of the speech, we will be more ready to look for similar features in the rest of it. Clearly the information gleaned here need be no inconsequential thing: it can be used to provide a key to our understanding of Hal and his role in the whole play. But for us here it is enough to see how once we become fully critical in the sense of taking nothing for granted, once we pay heed to every tiny nuance that troubles us, or take the time to consider closely for ourselves the words of the text, then quite unexpected facts may be revealed, and these facts may, first, permit us to come to our own free view of a work, and second, will often yield no trivial insight but provide a route to a new interpretation of the whole.

Still more may the critical faculty be silenced where we are faced by a text in which some authority, particularly that of the author, appears to tell us what to think. Once again we will need a certain amount of intellectual rebelliousness or courage, though here of a still more practised kind, to allow us to keep our critical distance and make up our own minds. In Pope's *The Rape of the Lock* a speech is given to one character, Clarissa, in which she indicts the entire trivial and materialistic society of Belinda, the mock-heroine of the poem, whose beauty is matched only by her folly. This speech was added to the expanded version of the poem in 1714, in order, Pope announces in a footnote '*to open more clearly the* MORAL *of the Poem*'. With this announcement we will be inclined to take it at face value and submit. The speech seems at first sight a plain piece of counsel to Belinda to base her life on more permanent and worthwhile values than the cultivation of her own beauty and power: beauty, she is told, is a transient thing, and it is better to look to 'virtue', 'good humour' and 'good sense', both to supplement our worth now and to see us through the time when 'Locks will turn to grey'.

Looked at more closely, however, the speech does not quite fit in with this seemingly generous counsel. In its first seven lines, it produces what amounts to a total indictment of beauty and its effects, asking,

> Say, why are Beauties prais'd and honour'd most,
> The wise Man's Passion, and the vain Man's Toast?
> Why deck'd with all that Land and Sea afford,
> Why Angels call'd, and Angel-like ador'd?
> Why round our Coaches crowd the white-glov'd Beaus,
> Why bows the Side-box from its inmost Rows?
> How vain are all these Glories, all our Pains,

Thus far, we would feel this to be a picture of beauty as mere vanity. Yet the next line runs,

> Unless good Sense preserve what Beauty gains.
> (Canto V, 9–16)

At first we may not see the discrepancy, but it is there. Seven lines of satire on beauty are followed by an eighth in which beauty is seen as gaining something worth having. Seven lines of seeming contempt for the world are followed by submission to it. Good sense is now not an alternative to beauty but a kind of support for it. This discrepancy is further underlined in the following couplet:

> That Men may say, when we the Front-box grace,
> Behold the first in Virtue, as in Face!

The very fops who seemed to be derided in the opening lines
as besotted and worldly fools, are now the source of applause
that should be sought. Now, it takes some time for the shift
in the speech to be noticed: it seems so assured, so certain of
its direction, that we are not going to look closely or give
much time to any twinges of uneasiness we may have felt. We
might be a little on our guard from factors outside the speech
though. We might recall that it was Clarissa who gave
Belinda's foe the Baron the scissors with which to cut off the
lock of her hair: is she as impartial as she appears here? –
might she not be jealous of Belinda and attack reliance on
beauty for that reason? And we may have felt that Pope
himself does not simply satirise Belinda, but also admires her
beauty throughout the poem.

At any rate, the discrepancy is there, and now that we have
seen it once we will look for more as Clarissa's speech
continues.

> But since, alas! frail Beauty must decay,
> Curl'd or uncurl'd, since Locks will turn to grey,
> Since painted, or not painted, all shall fade,
> And she who scorns a Man, must die a Maid;
> What then remains, but well our Pow'r to use,
> And keep good Humour still whate'er we lose?
> And trust me, Dear! good Humour can prevail,
> When Airs, and Flights, and Screams, and Scolding fail.
> Beauties in vain their pretty Eyes may roll;
> Charms strike the Sight, but Merit wins the Soul.

The first six lines seem elegiac, a sort of *memento mori*. Clarissa
seems to be talking about facing up to growing old, and
finding some inner value with which to do so. But then in the
last four she seems to have changed again, to be back with
the idea of using 'good Humour' as a way of winning other
people's applause. What seemed to be a process of finding
self-assurance becomes one of depending on outside acclaim.

And at the same time we see Clarissa returning to her patronising attack on beauty.

What we can do with these insights so far as interpretation of the poem goes is up to us. What we can say at this stage is either that Pope miscalculated, or that when he said Clarissa's speech was designed to open more clearly the moral of the poem he meant something rather more subtle than that she should simply be read without inspection of her credentials. If we take the latter course, then Clarissa will begin to appear as vain and trivial in her way as Belinda is in hers. And if this is the case, if the supposed moral mouthpiece of the poem undermines her own position, then we can advance to the proposition either that perhaps the moral of the poem is that the moralist has no place in it, or, more harshly, that the world of Belinda reduces all its inhabitants to its own image, rendering them vain and ethically impotent. Then we must test these propositions against the wider context of the poem.

But the point here is what can be done. By interacting with a speech rather than lying passive before it and any declarations made about it; by inspecting it in detail and testing its standards and consistency; and then by working towards a view of the character who utters it, and his or her presumed role, the character begins to have quite a different part to play in the poem from the one supposed. And when this happens, the work really comes alive for the reader, is at once his and yet is most objectively seen. We must always get through the complaisant blur which makes us accept what we are given. In short, we must be fully critical.

This business of being critical obviously goes beyond attention to speeches, though that is one of the easiest ways of showing it in action. It is equally applicable in the consideration of whole works, and in areas beyond those of discrepancies within passages. For instance, there is the area of seeming irrelevance. If we find one part of a work that seems to be irrelevant in relation to the rest, then this will provide us with scope for analysis. Why does Hardy spend so much time describing Egdon Heath at the beginning of *The Return of the Native*? Why does Fielding keep breaking up the narrative of *Tom Jones* with the prefatory chapters on his mode of writing at the beginning of every book? Or why, to linger a moment over one instance, does Chaunticleer the cock in

Chaucer's *The Nun's Priest's Tale* take so long and repeat his point so often when he is trying to persuade his lady Pertelote of the truth of dreams? He has himself dreamt of a beast that was about to eat him, and Pertelote has attempted to calm him by telling him that dreams are mere vapours produced by a bad diet or illness, which can be corrected with certain herbs which she bids him peck up. Instead he spends 200 lines of orotund pedantry citing authorities and recounting stories, all to prove the same point. Reading this, we could if we liked say that the speech reflects Chaucer's own interest in dreams, and consider its length no more; or we could assign it to the possibly pedantic interests of the teller of this tale, the Nun's Priest, which makes it rather more interesting. Still more, however, we could see it as a reflection of Chaunticleer's own character, and proceed to analyse that. For instance, its sheer length could suggest that Chaunticleer rather loses touch with the immediate subject, which is the terrifying dream he originally had. In fact if we look, we see that the speech becomes one in which he 'proves' that dreams in general can come true, rather than that his own dream will. It may then occur to us that in the course of his speech he becomes actually more concerned with defeating Pertelote in argument than with anything else: at the end of it, having 'won', he defies the medical remedies she has previously suggested, and patronises her. And also at the end he flies down from the beam where he has been talking, thus putting himself in direct danger of the very creature which originally started him on his long discourse. He even says, after taking so long to prove dreams true, that when he looks at Pertelote he defies 'bothe sweven and dreem'. If we have seen the 'irrelevance' here we may be able to perceive that it could reflect Chaunticleer's own 'irrelevance'; he has cut himself loose from the real facts of the world just as surely as his speech is cut loose from the rest of the poem. But seeing the irrelevance in the first place is the key, after which we can think through its implications.

Certain features in works of literature can work to encourage us to be critical. One is the critical mood itself within literature: that is, any form of irony or satire, by which we are invited to read below the immediate surface level. There can be obvious irony, where an evident fool or knave is being praised, as in Dryden's *Mac Flecknoe*, or Pope's *Dunciad*; or much more covert irony where, unless we are on our guard, we may find ourselves involved in the ironic process, as in Swift's satires. Another source of 'ready-made' criticism is the use in literary works of 'dramatised narrators', or tellers who have some evident bias in the way they present the story. Again, ready-made though they are, it is not always easy to spot their effect on a given story. Chaucer, to continue with him for the moment, uses them extensively in *The Canterbury Tales*, but while one might readily trace the embittered Merchant behind the cynicism of his tale, it would not so readily occur to us to assign the portrayal of truth in action and of love fused with marriage in *The Franklin's Tale* to the bourgeois indulgence of the Franklin himself. Quite often a narrator will be used to trick the reader into a complicity which he later learns to regret, as in some of Swift's satires, or in our sympathy with Conrad's Marlow in *Heart of Darkness* (where in the end he tells saving lies to himself and the world to protect himself from his own 'heart of darkness').

A striking instance of how energetically and perceptively we must work to be critical, even when we have a narrator before us, occurs in the novel *The Sacred Fount*, by Henry James. The novel is relayed to us through the perceptions of a narrator who remains nameless: this may the more persuade us to believe what he says, even not to be aware of him at all for some time. As a guest at a country-house weekend he meets some old friends whom he has not seen for a year or so – Gilbert Long, Mrs May Server and a Mr and Mrs Brissenden. We hear little of what they do or where they come from. To the narrator they all appear subtly changed. Since he saw her last Mrs 'Briss' seems to have grown younger and prettier; while he is shocked to see that Briss himself seems to have grown suddenly old. He is so struck by this that he begins to construct a theory involving what amounts to a process of spiritual vampirism, to explain it: for him Mrs Briss has fed off her husband's vitality and become younger, while Briss, thus drained, has aged. At the same time the narrator observes that Gilbert Long, previously quite dull, has become comparatively brilliant and witty. On the hint from another guest, Ford Obert, that May Server is rather more nervous and flighty than in the past, the narrator proceeds to build a theory based on his previous feelings about the Brissendens:

he decides that Gilbert Long is May Server's lover and that
their relation also is a vampiric one in which what is exchanged
is not years but intelligence, whereby May Server becomes
stupider than of wont, and Long brighter.

Try as he may the narrator can come up with very little
proof for these ideas: he has to support them by reading
volumes from the way people look or move, or by making
much of little moments of corroborating evidence from other
characters, or even by twisting the facts. Actually he is in a
way happier without direct proof: for him the world of the
unspoken is more real than that of the overt: he himself
virtually admits that if his theories became generally ratified
he would lose interest in them, 'Without suggestive evidence
there would be nobody in the house so conscientiously infernal
as . . . I' (ch. vii). But, for a good way into the novel, we are
prepared to take him at face-value, to accept what he infers
about these relationships and to grope like him for what
evidence there is. It does not quickly occur to us to question
his perception, since our attention is on the strangeness and
mystery of what he perceives. We ourselves are willing to
assent to his views, even to take his interpretation of Mrs
Briss's state from the carriage of her back as she at one point
moves away from him:

> Didn't what I saw strike me as saying straight *at* me, as far as possible,
> 'I *am* young – I am and I *will* be; see, *see* if I'm not; there, there, there!' –
> with 'there's' as insistent and rhythmical as the undulations of her fleeing
> presence, as the bejewelled nod of her averted brow?   (ch. x)

Certainly, though, the theory has become more convoluted
as the novel proceeds. The narrator sees signs of 'regeneration'
in May Server and of 'decline' in Long (in fact these may be
just the chance variations of character according to mood)
and decides that the vampiric relation is now going in the
opposite direction. Once more applying the 'torch of analogy',
as he calls it, he decides that the same must be true of
the Briss/Mrs Briss relation, and sets about detecting a
rejuvenation in the former and a decline in the latter. By this
point, however, we are at least potentially detached from and
critical of the way he applies a grid of theory to experience,
especially when one theory moves in the opposite direction

from an earlier one on the basis merely of innuendo or even of a love of neatness and symmetry:

> These opposed couples balanced like bronze groups at the two ends of a chimney-piece, and the most I could say to myself in lucid deprecation of my thought was that I musn't take them equally for granted merely *because* they balanced. Things in the real had a way of not balancing; it was all an affair, this fine symmetry, of artificial proportion. Yet even while I kept my eyes away from Mrs Briss and Long it was vivid to me that, 'composing' there beautifully, they could scarce help playing a part in my exhibition.   (ch. ix)

Or again, posing a possibility and then suddenly turning the possibility into a fact:

> If he [Long] was all wrong – if he, in any case, felt himself going so – what more consequent than that he should have wished to hide it, and that the most immediate way for this should have seemed to him, markedly gregarious as he usually was, to keep away from the smokers? It came to me unspeakably that he *was* still hiding it and *was* keeping away.   (ch. xi)

Perhaps we are not fully alienated from this at the time of reading, but are only awakened to our disturbance in retrospect: certainly there is a stage at which we still accept what the narrator says while becoming uneasy with him. Nevertheless the extent to which we do accept this without question is becoming the measure of our own capacity for self-deception.

James gives other clues to the suspect character of the narrator. The narrator loves his theories with a special and jealous love. 'For real excitement', he says, 'there are no such adventures as intellectual ones' (ch. ix). And he declares, '*I* alone was magnificently and absurdly aware – everyone else was benightedly out of it' (ibid). He is shown sympathising with and gesturing at helping the people he thinks are suffering, but in the end does nothing, realising that

> this was the price – the price of the secret success, the lonely liberty and the intellectual joy ... the special torment of my case was that the condition of light, of the satisfaction of curiosity and of the attestation of triumph, was in this direct way the sacrifice of feeling. There was no point at which my assurance could, by the scientific method, judge itself complete enough not to regard feeling as an interference and, in

consequence, as a possible check. If it had to go I knew well who went
with it, but I wasn't there to save *them*. I was there to save my priceless
pearl of an inquiry and to harden, to that end, my heart.   (ch. xv)

As he pieces together one aspect of his theory early on, he
reflects that '[it] fitted so completely to the other pieces in my
collection. To see all this was . . . to be as inhumanly amused
as if one had found one could create something. I had created
nothing but a clue or two to the larger comprehension I still
needed, yet I positively found myself overtaken by a mild
artistic glow' (ch. vi). The narrator, thus seen, is preying on
life to construct art. He hoards the supposed sufferings of his
subjects, speaking of 'my precious sense of their loss, their
disintegration and their doom' (ch. xiii). Looked at in this
way, the vampirism he sees in others is no less in himself: he
feeds off the lives of others too.

But this is not the whole truth, and if we make it so we can
become in a sense ourselves vampires, reducing the possible
elusiveness of life and art to a fixed theory. For we never learn
the truth: the narrator's theories may have been correct,
however questionable the manner in which he formulated and
pursued them: and certainly the novel is full of people making
the same kinds of theories, giving us the impression that
something strange really is going on, or else that Newmarch
(the country-house setting) has drawn to itself a remarkable
collection of artists *manqués*. Life is not more real than 'art',
or theorising: and to some extent the artist must always
distance himself from suffering and use it for his own purposes.
This is the larger ambiguity: we see that morally questionable
though the artist may be, he has to be questionable to be an
artist at all. Or a critic: for whatever we say about the novel
is a theory, however much we reduce its burden to the
indefinite.

Clearly this novel is founded on the reader being critically
alert: if he is not he shows himself as ignorantly assenting to
the questionable procedures by which the narrator carries out
his investigations. But equally the reader has to be alert to
his own alertness, as it were: he has to see the limitations of
the simply critical view of the narrator also. And even alertness
itself is led to its own limitations in the end – to the fact that
whatever we say, it too is 'only' a theory, and the work retains

its faintly mocking immunity. With most other works using 'dramatised' narrators it is sufficient for the reader to observe that the vision of such narrators is personal, biased or limited; but with James the 'critic as artist' is drawn in to find himself a kind of narrator, or theoriser, too.

Sometimes the conclusion of a work may be at variance with the rest of it, and this too, when we see it and inquire into it, can be a very fruitful way of being critical. In Ben Jonson's *Volpone*, for instance, we may feel that the end of the play, in which Volpone is unmasked for the schemer he has been, is not convincing. Volpone has shown himself a perfect trickster during the play, convincing a range of grasping would-be heirs that he is terminally ill and that each one of them is sole beneficiary of his vast wealth, a wealth which has been largely derived from the bribes they have been severally asked to pay to ensure his favour. Yet this 'fox', at the end of the play, decides to carry his trick to the limit, make it known that he is dead, and have Mosca, his 'parasite', made his sole heir, so that he may enjoy the discomfiture of those he has gulled for so long. This may seem to us the logical terminus to Volpone's schemes: since he has been pretending he is on the way to death for so long, why not take the final step in the trick? And this will normally silence our will to criticise. But when, as Volpone could readily have seen, the gulls turn against Mosca and seek to expose his previous criminal actions in court (which would if successful have led to the sequestration of Volpone's assets in the care of Mosca), he certainly criticises himself:

> To make a snare for mine own neck! And run
> My head into it wilfully, with laughter!
> When I had newly 'scaped, was free and clear!
> Out of mere wantonness! O, the dull devil
> Was in his brain of mine when I devised it.
>   (v.xi.1–5)

Even then he does not know that his scheme has also allowed Mosca to betray him. Again, instead of remedying matters as he might have by going to the court and saying that Mosca had locked him up and then made off with a forged will, he tries several schemes doomed to failure and is then exposed.

If we have felt the peculiarity of Volpone's behaviour here – and it has to be said that the plotting is complicated enough for us to lose our way – then we will be in a position to ask why, assuming there is a 'why', it is like this. The plain fact is that the moral laws of the comedy demanded Volpone's punishment: but we may hazard that the nature of Volpone as arch-manipulator made it unlikely that almost any piece of plotting by which he brought himself low could be convincing. Certainly we will find corroboration for our feelings here in Jonson's dedicatory Epistle to the play, where he admits that the obligation to punish vice in the play produced an unsatisfactory resolution of the plot which may 'meet with censure'.

Often, to remain critical and objective, we have to resist the internal pressure generated by a work to make us conform to a meaning which does not quite fit our experience of the whole. Here an example is Edward Albee's *Who's Afraid of Virginia Woolf?*, where the play may be felt to end on a note of togetherness and harmony between the previously warring married pair, which seems at variance with our sense of the energy and wit, however violent and destructive, generated by their previous discord. The couple, George and Martha, have previously sustained their illusions, and their mutual hostility, through the creation of an imaginary son: when George, finally goaded beyond endurance, 'kills off' this son, the way is open for the two eventually to accept the truth and with it, one another. It sounds wonderful, the kind of happy ending we would wish for: but is it so good? If we feel at all that the chastened, muted accents of the close seem a not quite adequate substitute for the vitality of the conflict that preceded them, then we will be on the way to a new view of the play, and an insight into the Albee who could write *A Delicate Balance*, or who could say through a character in his *The Zoo Story*,

'I have learned that neither kindness nor cruelty by themselves, independent of each other, creates any effect beyond themselves; and I have learned that the two combined, together, at the same time, are the teaching emotion. And what is gained is loss.'

The relation of George and Martha is more 'dialectical', we

may feel, more one of an interplay of opposites than the unitary kindness with which the play concludes. We may recall how once George expressed his fury at Martha's gibes by entering the room with what seemed terrifyingly like a shot-gun but which turned out when he pulled the trigger to be a trick gun with a Chinese parasol that opened as it emerged from the barrel. In a sense, it can be felt, their war was for them the true peace. Martha keeps talking about their set-to as a boxing match of wit in which each expects a good performance from the other. When George once comes in from the garden with a bunch of snapdragons, Martha screams, 'Pansies! Rosemary! Violence! My wedding bouquet!' If we have sensed a discrepancy in the ending of the play, if we have felt its true life in the war of wit that is put aside for 'mature self knowledge', and if we have the determination not to let the one impression be obliterated by the other, then we will see the play in quite a new light – perhaps itself as a kind of war or dialectic between the truth of the close and the earlier vivid illusion.

Already we have begun to see that 'getting critical' can involve finding weaknesses as readily as deeper strengths in texts. And if that is what is there, then there can be no reason for us not to say so. No *reason*, but plenty of fear. One of the greatest barriers to free criticism of literature is reverence. Equally one of the most depressing features of modern literary criticism is the prior assumption that certain writers can do no wrong. But we are not bound to say that Shakespeare never blotted or that Donne could not err: and if we think we are, by so much will we be unable to think clearly about them. Equally it is just as confining to approach some kinds of literature with a pre-cast contempt: the attitude of the literary establishment to science fiction is a case in a point. Any prior attitude inhibits the free play of the critical sensibility. But reverence is the commonest menace, since it turns critics into curators of the worthy deed, and students into parrots of acceptable opinions just when their minds are most flexible and creative.

The received opinion concerning Fielding's *Tom Jones*, for instance, is that it contains one of the finest plots in literature. We may not feel quite so enthusiastic. We might want to ask how it was that Tom Jones came to be turned off by his guardian Allworthy, for it is on that rejection, and on Tom's parting from his beloved Sophia Western, that the subsequent action of the novel depends. Allworthy is told by Tom's rival Blifil that when Allworthy was dangerously ill, Tom got drunk downstairs in expectation of his death and the money he would get. Actually Tom got drunk when he knew that Allworthy had recovered. When Allworthy then interviews Tom he never actually names why he is putting him out of the house. Fielding explains this as 'modesty', but this may not seem enough to us: had Tom known that Allworthy thought he had been celebrating his expiry rather than his recovery, he could at once have denied it. We might also want to ask why, after this rejection, Tom did not elope with Sophia Western. He loved her, and she him, and each knew it. Instead he takes final farewell of her and departs. There is no need for us to ignore this or to try to find reasons which will explain these difficulties: we can take them as plain weaknesses.

Then we may wonder at the solution to the plot. How is it that the tutor-philosopher Square, who has hitherto shown himself a cruel and hypocritical tyrant to Tom, should have it in him at all, even on his deathbed, to write a confession to Allworthy of Tom's true nature and goodness and of the plots laid against him? How can we accept Squire Western, once more as a lovable old 'hearty' at the end of the story, when the only thing that prevents him from being the foaming parental tyrant to Sophia he has been for the most of the novel is that Tom has become heir to Allworthy's fortune? Further, do we feel very happy that we should see Tom coming up to the standards of vulgar wealth and privilege in order to secure Sophia, instead of the manifestly too often corrupt holders of such privilege learning equality with their fellow man of whatever station? In a novel which for so long has dealt with Tom as a man of probably low birth, who spends much of his time in the company of common – and usually likeable – people, we may feel that the Christian or egalitarian assumptions on which such commerce seems founded are simply flouted by this ascent in rank. And if we have such feelings, we should not stop them. It may be that there are answers to some of those questions, but they must be convincing answers, and the questions should never cease to be asked.

This attitude of refusing to take valuations on trust should be applied to any writer. We should never start from unquestioned assumptions, but always keep in touch with the issues that raise themselves. Above all we should keep in mind the fact that writers are human, and rarely is anything they do perfect. The best praise we can give them is to see them for what they are. Might it not be possible to see Shakespeare's *Othello* to be a mere tissue of manipulations of plot by the author, from Othello's forgetting his having seen the handkerchief, to Cassio's omission of his mistress Bianca's name when he is talking bawdily of her to Iago, so that Othello can be persuaded he is talking of his wife Desdemona? And of Shakespeare, further: has Falstaff run away with the sympathies of his creator?; is the happy ending of *Twelfth Night* too facile a solution to the play?; does *Measure for Measure* fail to do justice to the issues of law versus mercy that it raises?; is *Coriolanus* a play of uncertain attitudes on Shakespeare's part?; is the evil in the late romances treated seriously enough for it to provide a real challenge to the benign drift of the plays? And if we find in favour of Shakespeare it must be convincingly so, and not by the erection of academic fences around sacred cows.

Again, how 'realistic' are the love-poems of John Donne? Is it not arguably the case that whenever Donne comes up against hard facts such as absence and death, and tries to show that they have no final power, as in 'A Valediction: forbidding Mourning' and Holy Sonnet X ('Death be not proud. . . .'), the arguments and images fail? Is it not conceivably the case that much of Donne's love poetry shows him in flight from fact, composing little universes of thought with which to oppose experience, as in 'The Flea'? And is it not possible to see his religious lyrics as an analogous flight from fact, in the way that in nearly every one of them Donne portrays his sinfulness as the product of inevitability and leaves his betterment to God's grace, not the exercise of his own will ('Good Friday, 1613. Riding Westward'; many of the *Holy Sonnets*)? Is Swift's *Gulliver's Travels* so much the satire it is made out to be, when much of it is concerned with pure fantasy, with such descriptions as how a giant and his possessions would appear to a diminutive race, how an island might fly, or how horses thread needles? Do the unlucky happenings in Hardy's novels strike us as mere manipulations to produce a gloomier outcome than is warranted whether in their world or ours? Is Evelyn Waugh's 'Sword of Honour' trilogy really the depiction of a changing attitude to war on the part of its anaemic hero, or is the hero's anaemia expressive of a lack of body and drive in the novels themselves? John Bunyan may have intended his *The Pilgrim's Progress* to be based on Calvinist theology, whereby the sinner is redeemed through God's grace alone and through no act of his own: but may we not equally feel, so clearly laid out is the obstacle race that Christian must run on his way to heaven, that every stage he passes is a victory of his will, and that he *earns* heaven? Is George Eliot's *Middlemarch* rightly sub-titled *A Novel of Provincial Life* when most of the main figures in it can be seen as highly untypical of Middlemarch, and the heroine Dorothea's history as the product not of 'a young and noble impulse struggling amidst the conditions of an imperfect state', but of herself and her choice of the cold pedant Casaubon as a husband? And so on; and much more.

So, now that we are sufficiently up and fighting, perhaps we can begin.

3
Close Analysis

This is not the place to try to teach by themselves and baldly all the various tools of close analysis of texts – attention to such features as rhyme, rhythm, diction, tone, imagery, syntax, alliteration and so forth. Other books have done this well enough. The purpose here is rather to show how one gets one's mind moving on the process of close analysis in the first place. What do we do when we are faced by the sudden 'thisness' of a text? How do we criticise it? How, with a longer text, do we select a passage that will give a good 'yield'? How do we relate our analysis of a passage to the wider context of the work from which it comes? One cannot hope to be comprehensive about this, but there are two very simple rules which, if backed up by practice in perception, will take us a long way. The most basic rule is to establish a rough meaning or direction if possible from within the text. The next is to observe the stylistic peculiarities, and fit the two together. As we do so, the meaning itself alters and becomes more manifold through our analysis.

Take the following for example:

> Below the thunders of the upper deep;
> Far, far beneath in the abysmal sea,
> His ancient, dreamless, uninvaded sleep
> The Kraken sleepeth: faintest sunlights flee
> About his shadowy sides; above him swell
> Huge sponges of millennial growth and height;
> And far away into the sickly light,
> From many a wondrous grot and secret cell
> Unnumber'd and enormous polypi
> Winnow with giant arms the slumbering
>   green.

> There hath he lain for ages and will lie
> Battening upon huge seaworms in his sleep,
> Until the latter fire shall heat the deep;
> Then once by man and angels to be seen,
> In roaring he shall rise and on the surface die.
> (Tennyson, 'The Kraken')

It is conceivable that one might begin analysing this as a mere arrangement of words without meaning, but one would not get very far. What we know of what the poem is about will be our starting point. Here the manifest subject is some great beast living far in the depths of the sea. It is the deepest of creatures: the sponges and polypi are above it. It has been there for ages and will not arise till 'the latter fire', the Last Days. It is not described, being simply 'the Kraken'; and it does nothing, only sleeps. Knowing that it is the deepest of beasts, we then may be more responsive to the syntax of the first four lines of the poem. For instance, the poem starts us with the 'upper deep', takes us below, then 'Far, far beneath in the abysmal sea': what we are heading for we do not know. The sense of suspension is continued in the third line, 'His ancient, dreamless, uninvaded sleep': we only arrive at the Kraken himself by the fourth line. For four lines the sense has been suspended, as we move through two prepositional phrases, and then through what might seem to be a subject but turns out to be an object, till we reach the true subject in the fourth. We can say that the sentence is arranged to pull us down, just as the sense does. The sentence lasts for four lines, and we await its point and the Kraken himself till we have been drawn down through the four lines to the depths of the ocean. But we do not stay with him there, for no sooner are we in the abyss than the poem pulls us back upwards to look above the Kraken to the 'Huge sponges of millennial growth and height', the last word taking us further upwards until we look 'far away into the sickly light' at the enormous polypi. The poem seems a continual movement of downwards and up. At the end it returns to the Kraken in the depths, to contemplate what will happen in the Last Days when he will rise to the surface. The imagery of the poem relates to different levels. We have the thunders of the upper deep (even that upper deep seems a throwing together of opposite movements), then (going down by going up) we have the polypi, the sponges and finally the Kraken.

The Kraken, however, we may then notice, does nothing: only sleeps and battens on huge seaworms. And we do not really *see* the Kraken: only hear of his shadowy sides, about which the 'faintest sunlights flee'. We can more readily visualise the sponges or the polypi, and if we ask why, we can see that it is because they are described vividly as doing something. When we read 'above him swell/Huge sponges of millennial growth and height', we can really feel what is being portrayed: and if we look we see that this is because the verb 'swell' occurs at a line end and before we know its subject, so that it as it were 'swells' into the next line. And this sense of dilation is continued in the way the sponges are depicted throughout the whole of that line – they seem to fill it. Or again there is the wonderful vividness of 'And far away into the sickly light,/From many a wondrous grot and secret cell/Unnumber'd and enormous polypi/Winnow with giant arms the slumbering green'. If we ask how this gains its power, we can say it is certainly something to do with that long last line: the verb 'winnow', strangely agricultural, comes at the start of the line and then seems to act almost without an object until the last word of the line; the 'giant arms' really seem to throw the line out wide with the adjectival extension so that we get a strong sense of the compass of the winnowing. But the whole four lines have been expansive because we have not known the subject nor the action being performed till we have read right through them. And we can carry that impression further if we think how we go upwards, 'far away into the sickly light', and then look at action in a horizontal plane, 'From many a wondrous grot and secret cell'. All this detail and powerful realisation contrast strongly with the obscurity in which the Kraken is left, in shadow or asleep.

So far so good. But if the poem is centrally about the Kraken, why is it given so little direct description? It is here that an intellectual jump must come: and not everyone will jump in the same direction; further, it will take critical practice and more than a first acquaintance with the poem to make the jump at all. The interpretation that follows here and the supposed reader response must be alike tentative, as with most of the interpretations in this book. Could it not be said, then, that the Kraken is the true subject of the poem because all these creatures, however huge, vital and various, however strongly realised, are only pale shadows of his reality? Around him 'faintest sunlights flee', reduced to mere minnows; he is the great reality to which the poem descends; and his awakening and arising will mark the end of all things. He need only be the Kraken: all other creatures have to do great things to be seen as great. He need not move to be a sort of prime mover. The 'there' with which his place is described after that of the sponges and polyps serves to include them within it. One of the contrasts we may notice in the poem is between the activity of the surface and the stasis of the depths. The upper deeps 'thunder'; the polypi 'winnow'; the sponges only 'swell'; the Kraken does nothing but sleep or batten in his sleep. (The fact seems heightened in the initial repetition of the word, apparently banal – 'His . . . sleep/The Kraken sleepeth'.)

At some point, if we have this idea of the vertical arrangement of the poem, with the undescribed and shadowy Kraken in the depths, it becomes possible now to think beyond the literal description of the poem and perhaps consider it as an image. After all, did the poet mean it simply as a portrayal of some mythical sea-monster? (By 'Did the poet mean' one intends here both conscious and unconscious meaning: the question arises from feeling that Tennyson must have had reasons, conscious or not, more than mere depiction for writing about such a creature.) The poem is enormously potent in its portrayal, and has so many complex patterns within it, that we are led to look further. More than this, the image it presents is one that can be highly suggestive. We go steadily downwards to a greater reality living in slumbrous darkness . . . . It will need no great jump of the practised imagination to see this as suggestive of the different layers of the mind, going down into the subconscious. After all, no-one can say what is in their subconscious – and can that not be linked with the way the Kraken cannot be described?

This reading of the poem in terms of mind is further prompted by its last lines. Why should Tennyson have talked about the Last Days at all, and why should he have portrayed the Kraken rising and dying on the surface? Fair enough about the Last Days, perhaps: he wants to show its near-eternity. But why the particular account of the dying? The Kraken's death seems in some way to be associated with its being on the surface, when its proper habitat is the deeps . . . . Could it not be argued that Tennyson is portraying the destruction of the unconscious when it is brought to light out of its native darkness? (Again, this is probably a view which will only become available after long practice and familiarity with such levels of reading.) The Kraken before was not seen save as a vast shadowy bulk, and it was concealed by the covering depths of the sea: now it is 'by man and angels to be seen', exposed to all, its privacy and secrecy lost. The Last Things will involve, as they do in the Bible, the opening and exposure of all things, of graves, of guilts, of the depths of the sea. But they will also involve an inversion and collapse of categories. Fire comes together with water to make the Kraken rise; the unconscious is driven into the conscious and dies. More than this, we can notice, if we follow this pattern of significance, that the Kraken acts for the first time at the end of all things, and of the poem: it rises and roars. But even as it acts it loses the capacity to act: it dies.

It might be possible to read still further than this: as for instance to ask whether Tennyson intended this poem as a praise of the unconscious and a warning of the dangers of scientific advance and the discovery of nature's secrets . . . . Or even whether the whole poem, if explained away by too rigid an exposure of its own secrets, will itself die. We could, again, read the imagery at another level, as a picture of the chain of evolution, apprehended by Tennyson without benefit of Darwin. Here we might see the present on the surface of things, reaching back through long ages of millennial growth' to the polypi, the sponges and finally to where the Kraken has 'lain for ages'.

But it is enough here to have shown how the sense of the poem's subject lights up aspects of the style, and then becomes further understood through awareness of other stylistic patterns, until the whole becomes a living and complex unity. 'Close analysis' is not a process that can be prescribed, nor is it one that uses all the techniques of stylistic investigation in any one instance. What one needs to look at is suggested both by the subject matter and by those peculiarities of style that jut out; and then insight comes from fitting them together.

Here what 'stuck out' was the syntax, the way the sentences were framed with delayed verbs, objects or subjects; and also the movement of the poem's description in a vertical direction, downwards, then up, then down, and finally up to the death of the Kraken. (We could add that much of the poem's energy comes from those continual changes of movement, and from the interplay of such vertical motion against horizontal action in the movements of the winnowing arms.) Thereafter consideration of adjectives and diction came in. But other tools of close analysis were not required.

Often close analysis can yield striking insights from the most ordinary-looking material; and the smallest and apparently most trivial of features can prove highly significant. An instance is the plain-seeming account in Milton's *Paradise Lost* of the moment when the still unfallen Eve leaves Adam despite his warnings and sets off on a gardening expedition. She has told Adam that she is and should be able to resist any temptation that may come to her, without the protection of Adam.

> Thus saying, from her husband's hand her hand
> Soft she withdrew, and like a wood-nymph light
> Oread or dryad, or of Delia's train,
> Betook her to the groves, but Delia's self
> In gait surpassed and goddess-like deport . . . .
> (Book IX, 385–9)

We know that Adam is reluctant to let her go, and that she is at once determined and nervous about resisting him. Thus it is appropriate that her action should be so delayed by the syntax, across the line end, 'Thus saying, from her husband's hand her hand/Soft she withdrew'. We are made more aware of the withdrawal of the hand because its mention seems slightly unexpected: after she had said what she did to Adam, and with the fairly brusque 'Thus saying', we might expect a simple description of her departure. The mention of hands here is, we may reflect, in such a context symbolic. Adam and Eve are parting, we know, in a more final sense, from one another; never again will they be so innocently close, so trusting as they have been; what marriage they have hereafter will be partly a divorce. But because of the singularity of the phrase here, the way the hands are emphasised by being thrown together at the end of the line, 'hand her hand' may perhaps remind us of other mentions, equally prominent, of their hands in the poem. When first we see them in Paradise they are 'hand in hand'. When we see them last on leaving it, they are also 'hand in hand', but now with a different kind of mutuality. Seen thus, this disjoining of hands here becomes the symbolic centre of the poem.

Then, if we are alert to the ominous element in Eve's departure here, words such as 'Soft' or 'light', each accentuated by being placed at the beginning and end of a line, take on rather more than a physical reference, become suggestive of the softness and lightness of character with which she will meet the serpent; and the softness may also express the instability of her obedience (as she has disobeyed Adam in a sense here, so she may disobey God), and the lightness her failure to grasp the seriousness of what she is doing. We may be put off by the oread, dryad and Delia: we have to know from the footnotes, if we do not already, that Delia is Diana. The most immediate fact we may know about Diana is that she is the goddess of chastity. Actually later in this passage we are to find Eve also being compared to Ceres, 'Yet virgin of Proserpina from Jove' (396). What we can say of this is that in a sense the temptation of her by Satan is described as a kind of seduction, his words described as entering her. So then the comparisons here to Diana and to her bettering of Diana, are to be felt as frail and poignant.

But as one reads the lines, one also notices another feature in them: the use of alliteration. Alliteration and other sound effects can often be given too subjective an interpretation, let alone presence, and one must be careful. Perhaps one begins to notice it with 'like a wood-nymph light'; and then other lines come forward – the 'd' sounds in the third and fourth lines, the 'g's in the fourth and fifth. Lastly, perhaps, because less strongly sounded, yet curiously much more present, are the 'h' sounds in the first line – 'her husband's hand her hand'. What do we make of these? Alliteration usually helps to bind words more closely together: but this is a context of parting, of disjoining. There is another way to see the various lines. The 'her husband's hand her hand' (and we must aspirate the 'h' sounds) slow down the line as we say it, giving it a pause, akin to the suspension of the syntax here, before the verb in the next line begins the activity. The pause conveys perhaps the reluctance on Adam's part, the carefully gentle movement on Eve's. We can even say that so many of these 'h' sounds together produce an effect rather like a sigh, as though the air were full of elegy.

The effect of the 'l's in the second line is by contrast undoubtedly to give the line an increased speed; and so it goes on as we career, almost in flight, through the succeeding lines of overlapping alliteration. To the production of that effect we might add the way the syntax after 'withdrew' is all one unit, and also the way that 'Delia', begun in the third line, is mentioned again in the fourth and contrasted with Eve in the fifth. This sense of sudden speed after the slow opening we can now try to explain. We can reiterate the gradualness of the separation of the hands and the different reasons for that on the parts of Adam and of Eve; and then we can say that the sudden speed thereafter imitates Eve's release, and her truant haste: it is, if we like, an imitation of abrupt gleeful freedom at the same time as it portrays her innocent quicksilver grace. At this point, aware of how the passage changes, and of its subject of release, we may notice something else. Each of the first four lines has a break of sense, or caesura, in it, marked by a comma. As we read the passage we may actually feel a sense of expansion: and if we look at where these commas come in the different lines we may see why. For if we count the number of syllables before them, through 'Thus saying', 'Soft she withdrew', 'Oread or dryad', 'Betook her to the groves', we will find that they go three, four, five and six, after which the sense goes over a whole line. This can readily be said to imitate the increasing release of Eve and her distance from Adam.

Now one may be amazed that so few lines can yield so much: but what we have found is 'really' there as data, if not the interpretations we have given them. Of course Milton in no way consciously intended any of the effects we have found: had he done so, they might well not be there. So long as we work from the evident meaning or mood of a passage and try to see how far this is reflected in its style, and so long as the stylistic effects we immediately attend to are the most striking ones, and ones demonstrably there, then we will be able to produce a convincing marriage of style and content and will probably also further our knowledge of both. But once again, what to attend to will be dictated by what is there, not by any arbitrary shopping list of qualities to be looked for in any text: some works will achieve their effects through certain devices, others through others. What has been shown here is just how minute and subtle the levels at which stylistic effects are achieved can be, how there is really no limit, where the text will warrant it, to the closeness of our inspection – so long as we are finding something that is there, not something we have put there. Above all, at this level at least, the possession of specialist critical knowledge is not the first requirement: what we need is the ability to see the stylistic features that matter, the patterns they form, and the significances they imitate and further. It is in itself a comparatively simple activity; but it does need much practice and persistence before results become recurrently obtainable.

One question that is often troublesome is how to find a passage that has so much yield in it in the first place. How do we know where it is? This would not so much be a question with 'The Kraken', for that is a whole poem: but still there remains the issue of how one chose that poem from among the many others of Tennyson; or indeed how any other of his poems comes to prominence while the rest are given less attention. Once again, the answer lies in what sticks out. So far as individual poems are concerned, one may feel when reading them that there is more mystery, power or subtlety in Tennyson's 'Lotos Eaters' or Hopkins's 'The Windhover' or Yeats's 'Byzantium' than in many other of their poems; and that is all there is to it. Of course, that leaves room for the discovery of neglected masterpieces or of flaws in the existing cynosures, or simply for disputes as to which are the best works, but that is not the issue: no insistence is being made here that some works are finally better than others, even if one feels so. It is up to the individual how much or little he or she finds in a work. And it should also be said that 'finding little', meaning finding little to say, does not make a work necessarily defective or limited: there are some works that by their simplicity, directness or mystery are simply not available to the techniques of literary investigation – some medieval lyrics, mystical poetry, for example. The fact that some texts may be more readily discussed than others does not make them better: but it may make them capable of yielding insights, whether into the mind of their creator or the larger work of which they may be a part.

So far as the discovery of 'significant' passages within a larger work is concerned, whether poem, play, novel or prose discourse, the criterion is again striking. In a play it may be a soliloquy, in which the central character's thoughts are gathered together in such a way as to throw uniquely concentrated light on him and themes of the play. In a novel it may often be a symbolic or descriptive passage: the portrayal of Egdon Heath in Hardy's *Return of the Native*, the picture of Hell in Joyce's *A Portrait of the Artist*, the passage describing the fog that begins Dickens's *Bleak House*. But often as we all know from sitting examinations where we are asked to write a commentary on a 30-line extract from a work, we can find quite unsuspected complexity and depth in passages we would never have considered central on our own. It is often a useful or salutary exercise for us just to take a passage at random from a work and practise with it to see what we can find in it. If the work is truly an 'organic' unity, then arguably any passage within it ought to be a subtly formed microcosm of that unity. This of course is only *ideally* the case: there really are many areas of a text which will yield less than others. But there is no need to dot the 'i's' and cross the 't's' here. Suffice it to say that in a novel or a play one can derive as much stylistic yield from a casual-seeming conversation as from a set-piece speech or description.

To show this, and some of the different techniques that can be employed in stylistic close analysis, here is a passage from Joyce's *Ulysses*. It occurs in the twelfth section, 'Cyclops', at the point where the Irish Jew Leopold Bloom, advertiser's agent and reflector of Dublin life, is in a bar where his presence and Jewishness are becoming the subject of attack from other drinking acquaintances. The narrator of the passage is himself one of the anti-semites; there is also a coarse citizen who is of the same attitudes as himself. Bloom has been asked what is his nation, and has declared, ' "Ireland . . . . I was born here. Ireland" ', at which the citizen spits in the corner and over

himself. There ensues a page of elaborate description of the
handkerchief he uses to clean himself: until,

– Show us over the drink, says I. Which is which?

– That's mine, says Joe, as the devil said to the dead policeman.

– And I belong to a race too, says Bloom, that is hated and persecuted.
Also now. This very moment. This very instant.

Gob, he near burnt his fingers with the butt of his old cigar.

– Robbed, says he. Plundered. Insulted. Persecuted. Taking what belongs
to us by right. At this very moment, says he, putting up his fist, sold by
auction in Morocco like slaves or cattle.

– Are you talking about the new Jerusalem? says the citizen.

– I'm talking about injustice, says Bloom.

– Right, says John Wyse. Stand up to it then with force like men.

That's an almanac picture for you. Mark for a softnosed bullet. Old
lardyface standing up to the business end of a gun. Gob, he'd adorn a
sweeping brush, so he would, if he only had a nurse's apron on him.
And then he collapses all of a sudden, twisting around all the opposite,
as limp as a wet rag.

– But it's no use, says he. Force, hatred, history, all that. That's not life
for men and women, insult and hatred. And everybody knows that it's
the opposite of that that is really life.

– What? says Alf.

– Love, says Bloom. I mean the opposite of hatred. I must go now, says
he to John Wyse. Just round to the court a moment to see if Martin is
there. If he comes just say I'll be back in a second. Just a moment.

Who's hindering you? And off he pops like greased lightning.

– A new apostle to the gentiles, says the citizen. Universal love.

– Well, says John Wyse. Isn't that what we're told. Love your neighbour.

– That chap? says the citizen. Beggar my neighbour is his motto. Love,
Moya! He's a nice pattern of a Romeo and Juliet.

Clearly it will not take us very far to look at this in terms of
syntax, rhythm or imagery: it is not so much the linguistic
style we must attend to but the interactions of the various
characters. It is through the analysis of the moral and
psychological complexities that the passage will yield results.
One sees this by starting perhaps with the observation of
one such 'complexity' and then looking for others. Enough
complexity is initially provided by the fact that an unsym-
pathetic character is describing Bloom: we have to see through
his point of view, see that while 'old lardyface' may in one
way be an apt description of Bloom, in another it is quite
unfair and inaccurate.

Suppose we go through the passage in detail, trying to

understand the interactions of the characters. It takes time to see it: but for this writer at least it seems reasonable to say that apart from Bloom the others appear to speak in clichés or empty figures: 'Show us over the drink', 'as the devil said to the dead policeman', 'Stand up to it then with force like men', 'Mark for a softnosed bullet', 'like greased lightning', 'A new apostle to the gentiles'. Bloom's language seems to come rawly and directly from his feelings. It breaks abruptly on the talk of drink, continuing the topic of Bloom's nationality, which he feels he has not yet defined adequately in calling himself Irish: his race is persecuted, 'Also now. This very moment. This very instant', as the Irish were persecuted in the past by the English. He is possessed by feelings the others misunderstand or scorn, and his nearly burning himself as he expresses it is reduced to dismissive contempt, 'Gob, he near burnt his fingers with the butt of his old cigar'. The layout of the passage, coming after a long descriptive passage, makes such phrases as 'Show us over the drink' and 'I belong to a race' come into contrast.

Looking over the whole passage in the light of them, it seems fair to say that Bloom's sense of 'belonging' or of nationhood is more generous than that of the others about him. Their Irishness is determined less by what it is than by what it shuts out: and here they are most of them intent on shutting out the Jew and feeling an ignorant sense of camaraderie. They hate and revile the unknown: they misunderstand what Bloom is talking about, perverting his pain at the sufferings of his race to a desire for a New Jerusalem, and at the end debasing his notion of love to cliché or incoherence. By contrast we can see that Bloom feels drawn out of himself to his people: he feels their pain calling to him. The mention of Morocco may remind us that his race has no country: unlike the Irish the Jews have no border they can draw about themselves.

But as we read the passage this contrast is not at first before us. When Bloom says, ' "And I belong to a race too . . . that is hated and persecuted. Also now. This very moment. This very instant" ', we can feel that the persecution that he is saying is happening now is also his own: he is partly talking about the way the people in the bar are getting at him for his Jewishness. But then, when he goes on to say that the

persecution he is talking about is taking place in Morocco we
can have two reactions. On the one hand perhaps we are thus
made aware that Bloom really is selfless (our thought that he
was disturbed at his own pains makes their true source come
over as all the more generous). On the other we may feel that
his pain *does* come from what he is suffering in the bar and
that his talk of the sufferings of his race in Morocco is a
sublimation or evasion of it. It is possible to sustain both
views of what Bloom is saying here, to see him both as moral
hero and as coward.

What then do we make of his reply to the citizen's asking
him whether he is talking about the new Jerusalem, '"I'm
talking about injustice"'? For his subject was not immediately
injustice: it was the other race he belonged to: the injustices
done to that race were incidental. This change of direction on
Bloom's part may give us further reason for supposing that
he has mixed and unacknowledged motives here: that he has
talked of the cruelties done to the Jews both for their own
sake and as a substitute for the cruelties done to him. We can
then go on from this to say that it is just this mixture of
motives that makes Bloom appear at once heroic and furtive
throughout this scene. Seen thus, a simple view of Bloom as
a heroic figure again will not suffice. When John Wyse says
that one should stand up to injustice like a man and then the
speaker describes Bloom as collapsing 'limp as a wet rag' into
a passive posture of forgiveness, we cannot wholly disagree
with the contemptuous view of him.

And yet at the same time, through all this cloud of
misunderstanding, that of those about him and his own,
Bloom is still saying and believing something truly valuable.
To the gospel of force, manliness and struggle he is opposing
that of love and forgiveness. If we look closely at his words:
'"But it's no use . . . . Force, hatred, history, all that. That's
not life for men and women, insult and hatred. And everybody
knows that it's the very opposite of that that is really life"',
we can see the words as perhaps an answer to everything,
that he is telling himself that anger is no use against the others
in the pub as much as he is talking about what will help his
people; and that he is also telling those about him that it is
useless to hate. In doing so he pays mankind a considerable
compliment. For we may ask whether everybody does know

that insult and hatred are the opposite of true life, given the previous and continuing behaviour of his companions to him: yet he is suggesting that in their hearts they do, that all men are really of good instincts, and out of self-respect will shun a life based on anything else. And then he goes out of the bar, just for a moment, to see Martin Cunningham about arranging a pension for Paddy Dignam's widow – an act of immediate charity which follows on from his statement of trust in love, however furtive and sneaking the situation and his behaviour may make the action look. Thus far Bloom, the passive hero, is truly there.

But then we have to ask ourselves how all this subject of love developed in a discussion where the issue is one's nationality. We know that there is an awareness in Bloom that he is being persecuted here: and it is to become overt later when he actively defies the other drinkers, while at the same time running away. We wondered how the topic of injustice developed out of that of belonging to a nation, and could see it as a concealed expression of Bloom's feelings of what is happening to himself here. His not sustaining his anger at the persecutors of his race could be seen as a failure to confront his own anger here as much as an act of love. In that sense the narrator with his view of him as collapsing and going limp would be again partly right. After all, we may ask how Bloom can say, 'That's not life for men and women, insult and hatred', when it is precisely that that he has been showing to be the inevitable lot of his own race. We may reflect that he has lost touch with what he was saying: again because 'what he was saying' was not entirely his true subject. Underneath, a mixture of cowardice and charity at his own pain here is driving him to go back on his own anger to make his declaration of love and eventually leave the scene. And we may well be struck by the way he puts that declaration – '"Love," says Bloom. "I mean the opposite of hatred"'. It can sound extraordinarily naive or clumsy. Do we not know what love is without having to be told it by its opposite?

And yet, we may reflect, perhaps we do not know what love is and certainly those about Bloom do not. And perhaps there is a point in putting it this way. After all, everyone about him is obviously ready to misconstrue the word. By putting it as 'the opposite of hatred' he makes it a feeling, an emotion, not a principle, like the principle of universal love or love thy neighbour to which others would turn it. We realise that Bloom means a real liking for people, a loving of them for themselves, whatever happens, however useless the love may be. And we have seen enough of his love for all things, the most lovely and loathsome, during all his lengthy perambulations about Dublin, already described at length, to know that he really does like all things for themselves, that he harbours no grudges, that he really does think well of his fellow man, however much he himself may often be sordid, furtive or evasive.

This is one way of analysing the scene. Clearly it leaves aspects of it out; and clearly too there will be other ways of looking at it. But centrally such a passage and situation call for an analysis of character and motive through the language and what is said. As with everything else we began with what stuck out: here it was Bloom breaking in on the clichés over the distribution of drinks with an abrupt statement of personal feeling. Then we were led to look at the interplay of the clichéd and the direct throughout the scene, and to relate that to attitudes to emotion and to openness of heart generally. Then we considered other aspects of the scene that brought themselves to notice, particularly the way Bloom's statement of belonging switched to a sense of the wrongs done to his people; thence to the sense that the force and hatred that might remedy this are futile; and finally to a praise of love. We could relate these changes in direction to an unacknowledged mixture in Bloom of anger, fear and love at the persecuted situation in which he finds himself in the bar. So the principle of investigation is the same: having established the prime subject or concern, which is here the interaction of character, the expression of self through language and moral analysis, we then moved on to the 'prominences' of the passage and worked outwards from there. These and any other prominences are if we like forms of the 'disjunctions' discussed in a later chapter: it is part of any critical activity to start with what strikes us most and go on from there to try to see how it can be seen ultimately to fit with the surrounding material. None of the special categories in this book – 'disjunction', 'structure', 'comparison', 'connection', is a special tool employed only on certain occasions: each is the staple of critical analysis at all times, though there will be occasions when one of them forms the prime method of investigation.

Quite a different mode of analysis may be called upon in considering another area of the same text: certainly *Ulysses* is various enough for this to be so. There is no fixed *a priori* method, only what is asked in one place and maybe not in another. But the ways in which we analyse prose are not, apart from such features as rhyme, enjambment and metre, markedly different from those used with poetry. Take this passage from *Ulysses*: it occurs in the first section, called 'Proteus', where Stephen Dedalus, the young intellectual exile returned, is on the beach near Dublin on the morning of 16 June 1904 wondering (à la Berkeley) whether the world, the 'ineluctable modality of the visible', will have disappeared when he closes and then opens his eyes:

See now. There all the time without you: and ever shall be, world without end.

They came down the steps from Leahy's terrace prudently, *Frauenzimmer*: and down the shelving shore flabbily, their splayed feet sinking in the silted sand. Like me, like Algy, coming down to our mighty mother. Number one swung lourdily her midwife's bag, the other's gamp poked in the beach. From the liberties, out for the day. Mrs Florence MacCabe, relict of the late Patk MacCabe, deeply lamented, of Bride Street. One of her sisterhood lugged me squealing into life. Creation from nothing. What has she in the bag? A misbirth with a trailing navelcord, hushed in ruddy wool. The cords of all link back, strandentwining cable of all flesh. That is why mystic monks. Will you be as gods? Gaze in your *omphalos*. Hello! Kinch here. Put me on to Edenville. Aleph, alpha: nought, nought, one.

Spouse and helpmate of Adam Kadmon: Heva, naked Eve. She had no navel. Gaze. Belly without blemish, bulging big, a buckler of taut vellum, no, whiteheaped corn, orient and immortal, standing from everlasting to everlasting. Womb of sin.

Wombed in sin darkness I was too, made not begotten. By them, the man with my voice and my eyes and a ghostwoman with ashes on her breath. They clasped and sundered, did the coupler's will. From before the ages He willed me and now may not will me away or ever. A *lex eterna* stays about Him. Is that then the divine substance wherein Father and Son are consubstantial? Where is poor dear Arius to try conclusions? Warring his life long upon the contransmagnificandjewbangtantiality. Illstarred heresiarch! In a Greek watercloset he breathed his last: *euthenasia*. With beaded mitre and with crozier, stalled upon his throne, widower of a widowed see, with upstiffed *omophorion*, with clotted hinderparts.

How do we get our bearings with this? Perhaps the first thing to do here is to try to grasp the basic subject or content of the passage. Here we can say we have a picture of the movement of Stephen's mind as it works on what he perceives. He has just tried to see whether the world goes away when he shuts his eyes, and still finds it very solidly there when he opens them. It may strike us that the fact is made all the more forcibly by the abrupt shift from subjective to objective narration, and from the portrayal of Stephen's thoughts to the actions of others, 'There all the time without *you*', '*They came* down the steps from Leahy's terrace'. We could say further that these others seem still more physically present in the sentence, 'They came down the steps from Leahy's terrace prudently, *Frauenzimmer*: and down the shelving shore flabbily, their splayed feet sinking in the silted sand'. Quite apart from *what* is described, the shelving shore, their flabby movement, their splayed feet sinking, the silted sand, there is the way the syntax is left as it were to sink through adverbial phrases, with the subject and verb left behind, and the heavy use of alliteration on 's'. For a time we stay with them: then we see a change as Stephen's mind gets to work on them, turning them into a sisterhood with a bag containing an abortion; and then we are wholly back inside his head as he begins to speculate on navels. So the first 'sighter' we have on the passage is that the inner world of mind and the physical world of bodies are the subject: Stephen has just been asking whether the outer world is real, and now we have the interplay between its reality and his pattern-making mind.

Then we look at other oddities that occur in the passage – no shortage of them here, indeed so many that it may seem hard to find sense from them. The first and most evident in Stephen's amazing idea of all humanity linked back to the first humans, Adam and Eve (though he prefers to stress Eve), through their navels: he moves from this to imagine all the linked navels as a kind of telephone exchange through which one might dial the garden of Eden. Why this image? We can say it is Stephen playing with ideas: midwives lead to misbirths, lead to navels, lead to all men descended through their navels, lead to the equation of navels with telephone lines. How seriously, for example, can we take the 'That is why mystic monks' here? It is a very oblique way of putting it, but if we think hard of why it has come up in this context we will see that Stephen is talking about the cords around the monks' cassocks, and likening these to navel cords. Such an idea seems purely whimsical. And yet there may be point in Stephen's thoughts here. Is he creation from nothing or is he joined to others? Is the world in his head or is it separate from him? Here we are beginning to put the separate strange items of the passage together. (And we may remark at this point that our *critical* making of links is another form of that struggle for significance that Stephen is making.)

Why do these questions of connection matter to Stephen? He has, the novel has earlier told us, refused his mother's last wish, that he pray for her on her deathbed. He is back with that larger mother he rejected and left, his native land of Ireland, trying to make sense of the fact. Fastidious and alone, he yet needs to belong. Thus, we may say, his thoughts lead him to contemplate with some love his imagination of the first mother; thus, equally, his thoughts then drive him to a sense of corruption, to the picture of the womb of sin. The latter part of the extract seems darker in mood. The picture of his engendering is one of a random and loveless conjunction: no linkage here, we might say. He goes on, speculating about the relation of fathers and sons. God, not his parents, decreed his birth. Does that not involve a form of consubstantiality between the son and the father? His thoughts swivel naturally to the heretic Arius, who (we will find if we look him up) maintained the separation of the Father and the Son, but in portraying Arius's failure Stephen seems himself fascinated by it, drawn to that bejewelled and sordid end he portrays. The divine link remains unmade; the decree that made him leaves him fatherless, parentless, sin-bound.

By now we seem to have a rough pattern for the extract which actually revolves about the three paragraphs. In the first section Stephen is trying to make links and patterns and goes back in time to find the first cause. Then in the middle paragraph he is still, contemplating that fruitful beginning. But in the last he on the whole traces the decay of connections – perhaps the emphasis on sin increases the sense of separation. Thus we can see the whole extract as roughly symmetrical, with the central paragraph on Eve as pivot. And the whole could be said to be unified, in that Stephen's sequence of thoughts is making connections among separate phenomena, and it is *about* connections, and we are making connections in observing this pattern . . . and beyond that God has made the pattern of connection that will necessarily produce Stephen . . . .

And by now, with an awareness that the second part of the extract is rather in contrast to the first, we may see other differences. Down to Eve, Stephen talks about women and the mother. Thereafter, the subject is the relation of father and son, and we are left with the dried-up male Arius. Then we might see that while Stephen talks about life and creation in the first part, the emphasis in the second is on death, sterility and decay. Stephen's recurrent mention of the mother reminds us of his torn feelings about his own mother. As for the whole passage, it seems to begin and end stuck in the physical, from the splayed feet of the midwives sinking in the sand to Arius struck rigid in his watercloset with 'clotted hinderparts': the rest of it we can see as an attempt by the mind to transform bleak, separated reality, in the vision of Eve and interconnection, before falling through Stephen's vision of his disjoined parents to that of the disjoiner Arius. Even so, the whole extract is also a journey into mind: Stephen looks for a time at what is happening on the beach and then moves away from it into his head until by a series of mental leaps he is completely removed from the original stimulus. (He, if we like, has defeated what he sees as the 'ineluctable modality of the visible' in the world by making an entirely new mental world.) So we have a dual impression: the passage is highly 'mental', and yet at the same time the thoughts are all entwined with the physical, in a mixture of fascination and loathing. And that, we can say, captures Stephen's dual nature, wishing to escape Ireland, his mother, his body, yet absorbed in them, drawn to them, drawn even to their repulsiveness. Beyond all this we could, if we recall that the section from which this passage is taken is called 'Proteus', link its changes, the way one thing continually turns to another with the protean changes of the god himself, especially as portrayed in the *Odyssey*, of which this book is intended to be a modern version.

Something like this we could say with what is certainly a difficult passage: but the point is that we arrive at being able to say it at all by taking what is prominent, asking why it is, and moving on to make further links until we have a grasp of what basically is going on in it and why those thoughts and images are occurring in this way and in this sequence. It is possible to draw quite different conclusions from the passage: this reading is only a tentative one. Nor does it cover everything that is there. For instance it says nothing of the literary allusions that run through it. Here only lengthy literary experience or very thorough annotation will help us. In the sixth line, 'like Algy', is, we must believe, a reference to the poet Algernon Swinburne and his view of the sea as 'mighty mother'. 'Will you be as gods?' refers to Satan's temptation of man in Milton's *Paradise Lost*. 'Whiteheaped corn, orient and immortal, standing from everlasting to everlasting' is an adaptation from one of the *Centuries* of the seventeenth-century poet Thomas Traherne. Doubtless there are others. Even these we only see after much reading of literature. In themselves as a matter of fact they do little. As literary allusions, however, we could link them to the theme of interconnection that runs through the first part of the extract where they occur: they serve to link Stephen's thoughts with those of others, just as he is trying to make links with all men here. What, looking elsewhere, do we make of the 'Aleph, alpha'? 'Aleph', if we look it up, is Hebrew for 'one', and 'alpha' is Greek for 'one'. By putting them together could we not argue that Stephen is fusing them – go further, is he not perhaps bringing together Greek and Hebrew civilisations in this gesture? (Later, in the 'Nighttown' section we will find Stephen's philosophy satirised in the saw, 'Jewgreek is greekjew'.) If we think out to the whole passage we will see that his whole thought is founded on a mixture of philosophic (Greek?) speculation and Hebrew mythology. Bringing the two together here fits with the theme of interconnection also. This then would explain too why Adam is called not just Adam but 'Adam Kadmon', and Eve 'Heva'.

Beyond all this of course there is the sheer terrifying vigour of the passage, unanalysable, seen in the images of the misbirth 'with a trailing navelcord, hushed in ruddy wool', the great blemishless belly changing from vellum to corn, the 'ghostwoman with ashes on her breath', Arius on his water-closet (perhaps we contrast the later and happier picture of

Leopold Bloom on his) 'with upstiffed *omophorion*, with clotted hinderparts'. The passage is as much full of a delight in words as in the patterns of significance to be made of them. We may relate this if we like to Stephen's relative detachment from the world – and compare it with the (contrastive) immersion in phenomena that we see in the character of Bloom; but still we are left with an elemental delight in language as in the world itself, that we can find throughout *Ulysses*. Still more, we may well feel that the meaning of the passage still dances beyond us: but that is the life of it, that is what draws us still further towards it. What is an omophorion? A lovely word, certainly. Why exactly do we have that picture of the death of Arius? What is the meaning of the very long word on which Arius wars his whole life long? Why was Stephen 'made not begotten'? Why does Eden have the telephone number Stephen gives it? If we knew the answer to everything, if we could find a reason for all the astonishing particularity of the passage, it might through all that explanation become a mere dead thing.

It may occur to us that Stephen himself does not know all that he is saying. The vigour of the passage comes also from the fact that this is a stream of consciousness (though conducted in the context of a conscious philosophic question about the world): one thought prompts another naturally rather than artificially, as much through association as through argument. Stephen finds his way to Eden as readily through accident as by design, as much by the local and accidental promptings of images as by any foreseen discourse. And it is at that unconscious level, as much as at the conscious one, that we are asked to respond to the images, becoming in some degree identified with Stephen's mind as it moves, with the very process of the intellectual surge and sweep as much as with the products of that movement.

Any given passage from a work will dictate the terms of the investigation into it. Sometimes it will ask attention to language, sometimes to imagery, argument, psychology, morals, sometimes to several of these at once. When we know what we are looking for in this area, then we notice the peculiarities of the passage, the items that jut out or do not quite fit, and we work from them to see the patterns within the passage, and to make connections with other items, until the whole thing reveals connections of which we could not at first be aware. It sounds simple: in the end it is relatively simple and certainly enriching to one's response to literature. But it needs practice, practice, practice.

4
Close Analysis as an Interpretative Key

Very often the close examination of a passage will provide insights that we can take beyond the passage itself to widen out into the work as a whole. This process of finding 'parts' lead out to 'wholes' is the one we find in the analysis even of the individual passage where, as we have seen we start from some striking feature and work outwards to link others to it. But equally, it can be just as fruitful to work back from our sense of the whole to a deeper understanding of the part. This two-way process, by which the local passage and the text as a whole can become mutually illuminative will be our subject here.

As example consider this speech by the king in Shakespeare's *Richard II*. He has not been a popular king because of his heavy taxes and luxurious court, and when he returns to England after wars in Ireland, it is to find a rebel army, under the formerly exiled Henry Bolingbroke, mustered against him. Further, his own support begins to melt away from him: the Welsh assistance he expected for his army is gone and much of the country is described as in arms under Bolingbroke. Richard also learns that Bolingbroke has executed his favourites Bushy, Bagot and Green. When one of his followers begins to ask the whereabouts of the Duke of York and his army, supposed supporters of the king, Richard breaks in with

No matter where – of comfort no man speak.
Let's talk of graves, of worms, and epitaphs,
Make dust our paper, and with rainy eyes
Write sorrow on the bosom of the earth.

Let's choose executors and talk of wills:
And yet not so, for what can we bequeath
Save our deposed bodies to the ground?
Our lands, our lives, and all are Bolingbroke's,
And nothing can we call our own, but death
And that small model of the barren earth
Which serves as paste and cover to our bones.
For God's sake let us sit upon the ground
And tell sad stories of the death of kings:
How some have been deposed, some slain in war,
Some haunted by the ghosts they have deposed,
Some poisoned by their wives, some sleeping killed,
All murdered – for within the hollow crown
That rounds the mortal temples of a king
Keeps Death his court, and there the antic sits,
Scoffing his state and grinning at his pomp,
Allowing him a breath, a little scene,
To monarchize, be feared, and kill with looks,
Infusing him with self and vain conceit,
As if this flesh which walls about our life
Were brass impregnable; and, humoured thus,
Comes at the last, and with a little pin
Bores through his castle wall, and farewell king!
Cover your heads, and mock not flesh and blood
With solemn reverence; throw away respect,
Tradition, form, and ceremonious duty;
For you have but mistook me all this while:
I live with bread like you, feel want,
Taste grief, need friends – subjected thus,
How can you say to me, I am a king?

(III.ii.144–77)

The reaction of the Bishop of Carlisle to this speech is 'My lord, wise men ne'er sit and wail their woes, / But presently prevent the way to wail'. And certainly, while we may feel that Richard had some justification in being despondent at the outset of his speech, by the end we may feel he has indulged that despondency too far. He still has an army with him: why give up, why not make a fight of it? And how does he go about giving up? Not in the ordinary way, it seems not by talking about the enormous odds against him, but by uttering a long speech on death. He seems to have lost touch with the cause for the speech and to debate issues that have nothing directly to do with his situation – what he has to leave in his will, the inevitability of violent death for kings, the idea that he is not really a king at all. Perhaps even the fact that this is so long a speech is what at first alerts us to this idea of Richard's losing touch with events: he goes off into a long mental exploration which ceases to be part of the conversation before and after it: we can almost picture his supporters standing about him in puzzlement and possibly alarm as he goes on, into ever more separation from them, and ever more despair.

And if we consider the play as a whole we will find Richard often doing this sort of thing: suddenly giving vent to long and rambling soliloquies. But we may also reflect that the Richard we saw in the first two acts of the play, when he was overseeing and eventually stopping a trial by combat, and when he was opposing John of Gaunt, seemed a much more distant and resolved figure than he appears here. There we did not see far into his inmost thoughts: here, he seems intent on making such thoughts primary. We have moved, if we want to put it more conceptually, from a public to a private Richard. Privacy to some extent is what this speech is about: Richard is saying he is not king but mere man, with man's needs.

So much by way of general considerations: now for the speech itself. First he says, 'Let's talk of graves', and then within a line we find him talking about actually writing his sorrow on the dust around him with the water from crying. The image is a fantastic one: and it is one that seems to play with the situation. Whatever Richard really feels seems rather lost here in what feels like an indulgence, a pleasing image he makes for himself. Why is he talking about death? And what about his picture of the deaths of kings? If we are already critical of the way he is speaking, we may turn over in our minds his statement that all kings are murdered: and will then realise that it simply is not true, for many kings have died of illness, accident or old age, from William the Conqueror to King John. Why then is he saying they have been murdered? Out of self-pity? And does he even keep to the point? For when he talks of death allowing kings a little time to monarchise and feel important, as if flesh were impregnable, and then coming with a little pin to ruin all, it may occur to us that he could as readily be talking about death by natural causes as violent death – indeed that his subject has now changed from the murder of kings to their perishability. What were sad stories about the deaths of kings have become a picture of death's power.

And by now we may be led to more overt awareness than we otherwise might have concerning the changes of subject that seem to take place in the speech. First Richard says: 'Let's talk of graves, of worms, and epitaphs'; then instead of talking about them, he has a picture of being sorry and writing one's sorrow in the dust. Then he comes back to discussion of death, but resolves instead to talk of another aspect, that of making wills; yet immediately he says that this would be futile, since there is nothing to leave as Bolingbroke has taken it all. So he starts on a new tack: let us 'tell sad stories of the death of kings'. Presumably we feel the reason for this to be that he can then feel part of a sad fraternity. He is at first, we think, talking of some kings who have had sad stories; indeed the word 'some' recurs; but when he draws the conclusion 'all murdered', the generalisation is unjustified as applied to all kings. But we can see how he got there: he was so absorbed in listing the different sad ways in which the wretched kings with whom he feels sympathy ended, that he comes to believe that he is talking about all kings. But what we can deduce from this is an inability to keep in touch with reality, whether it is with facts themselves or even with the facts of his own argument. Thus we see him move on to another subject where, instead of talking of the murder of kings, he is speaking of the inevitability of death's action on them in presumably any form. Lastly, he tries to pretend he is not a king at all, but a man like other men. At first he said kings were special marks for murder, then that death always got them in the end: he has been led by what must now seem his own grasshopper mind into saying that death levels all and therefore a king is no different from the next man. So the whole speech is made up of a mass of embroiderings more or less irrelevant not only to the issues immediately in hand but to one another. We can say the speech lacks as much unity and purpose as Richard himself seems to at this juncture in his career.

But beyond this we are led out by it to a further understanding of the make-up of the play of which the speech is a part. In the first place its very existence gives us, as we have seen, a private Richard in contrast to the more public one of earlier acts. He is intent throughout the speech on being nothing but private, even on ceasing to communicate with anyone but himself. 'Let us . . .' is solipsistic: his whole object is to display and luxuriate – for if we consider the time he takes over his miseries, 'luxuriate' is the word – in his innermost feelings. The fact that we have a public and 'ceremonial' Richard in the first part of the play, and one who in the rest does anything to pretend he has no ceremony, seems to suggest some sort of dualism not just in his portrayal but in the fabric of the play as a whole.

And if we think of the portrayal of Bolingbroke, Richard's opponent, we may be able to extend the point. For Bolingbroke is depicted as not thinking very much. He is the man of action, constantly engaged in doing: Richard says of him later, 'They well deserve to have / That know the strong'st and surest way to get' (III.iii.200–1). Bolingbroke is very much integrated with reality. He does not speak soliloquies, but always addresses others. When in the first act he is exiled to France for six years, and his father Gaunt tells him to use his imagination to make his exile seem a happy time by transforming its grim reality to pretty pictures in his mind, Bolingbroke replies scornfully, 'O, who can hold a fire in his hand / By thinking on the frosty Caucasus? / Or cloy the hungry edge of appetite / By bare imagination of a feast?' (I.iii.293–6). Aware of how much Richard uses just this sort of thought and imagination, if to make things gloomier rather than happier, these words of Bolingbroke's will come more readily to mind: and if they do we will have added authentication for the contrastive picture we are beginning to have of Bolingbroke as doer and Richard as thinker.

And there is more. The play leaves certain questions concerning Bolingbroke's behaviour unanswered. Did he intend to usurp Richard and become king? Did he subsequently intend that Richard should be murdered? In the play there is at least as much evidence that these things happened rather than were planned: Richard in a sense almost gives him the throne, makes him take it; and the murder of Richard is carried out by someone who drew his own inferences from some oblique words let slip by Bolingbroke at one time, inferences which Bolingbroke subsequently repudiates, while accepting that he is inevitably implicated in the guilt of the death. In one way it is possible to see Bolingbroke almost as having no motive at all, thus reinforcing our picture of the doer/thinker, body/mind duality between himself and Richard.

But, with practice and hard thought, we can take the contrast further. Why, we asked, is Richard talking about death so much in this speech? True, he has a prophetic intuition of his own end. But it is clear from the speech that he is half in love with the subject: it calls forth his greatest energy, his most elaborate flights of thought. He latches on to the topic at once as soon as he hears things are against him: no gradual descent into despair for him, but an immediate and forthright 'Let's talk of graves, of worms, and epitaphs'. He spends the whole speech telling us how ephemeral life is – all his possessions are gone, all kings are hollow men, all flesh is grass. Later as said we are to find him almost giving away the kingship to Bolingbroke. In another soliloquy he proposes to give away all he has and be buried in 'a little grave, / A little, little grave, an obscure grave' (iii.iii.152–3). He abdicates by a process of stripping, which once again ends with him picturing his own extinction (iv.i.200–18). He says, 'I must nothing be' (iv.i.200). Putting all these facts together, we might say that Richard has. a kind of reductive mania. He really seems to want to be dead, to be nothing. As the king we see in this soliloquy he is not sure of himself. And by 'sure of himself' we can mean 'sure of his identity': he does not know who he is. In a soliloquy prior to this one when he came ashore from Ireland to oppose the rebels, he could talk in preposterous terms of his mere kingly presence frightening them into flight (iii.ii.36–62); here he sees his kingship as nothing but a sham, a hollow crown. Because he has lost touch with himself we might say – and could say that this is emblematised in the way that we see a 'public' Richard in the first acts of the play and a purely private one here, as though his two selves are disjoined – because of this loss of contact with the self, he is bound to look for the correlative of that sense of nothingness in death. He is fascinated by death, we can say, because he feels that he has no hold on life and wants to go to death because there alone he will be truly what he is.

But we can go wider than this sort of – perhaps complicated – psychological interpretation. Bolingbroke acts, we said, and Richard thinks: but more than this, Bolingbroke acts and Richard is passive. And that is something we see with Richard in every different context of the play except at his end. He prevents the early combat of Bolingbroke and Mowbray going forward: just when the fight is about to begin he halts it. When he returns from Ireland he may speak of his regality striking down his foes, but it is his regality – or, later, the land itself – that will do it, not he. He will not have to lift a finger. And here, when asked to bend his mind to action, he sinks away from it, desirous we may even say only of that ultimate image of passivity, death. After this he makes no resistance to Bolingbroke: indeed we can see his relation to Bolingbroke as a curious one in which Richard's inactivity could seem to make Bolingbroke the more active. But the reason for Richard's being passive where Bolingbroke is active will not be attributable only to psychological differences but as we began to see elsewhere, to a kind of metaphysical split in the play, whereby nobody can be a whole man and there is a sort of radical dualism between thinking and acting, mind and body.

The analysis of the speech from *Richard II* was based on such criteria as relevance and the reasons for the subject of the speech. Other intuitions might start from quite different apprehensions; or they might work back from the text into the speech as much as the other way round. Consider the opening to Dickens's novel *Hard Times*, a chapter called 'The One Thing Needful':

> 'Now, what I want is, Facts. Teach these boys and girls nothing but Facts. Facts alone are wanted in life. Plant nothing else, and root out everything else. You can only form the minds of reasoning animals upon Facts: nothing else will ever be of any service to them. This is the principle on which I bring up my own children, and this is the principle on which I bring up these children. Stick to Facts, sir!'
>
> The scene was a plain, bare, monotonous vault of a schoolroom, and the speaker's square forefinger emphasized his observations by underscoring every sentence with a line on the schoolmaster's sleeve. The emphasis was helped by the speaker's square wall of a forehead, which had his eyebrows for its base, while his eyes found commodious

cellarage in two dark caves, overshadowed by the wall. The emphasis was helped by the speaker's mouth, which was wide, thin, and hard set. The emphasis was helped by the speaker's voice, which was inflexible, dry, and dictatorial. The emphasis was helped by the speaker's hair, which bristled on the skirts of his bald head, a plantation of firs to keep the wind from its shining surface, all covered with knobs, like the crust of a plum pie, as if the head had scarcely warehouse-room for the hard facts stored inside. The speaker's obstinate carriage, square coat, square legs, square shoulders – nay, his very neckcloth, trained to take him by the throat with an unaccommodating grasp, like a stubborn fact, as it was – all helped the emphasis.

'In this life, we want nothing but Facts, sir; nothing but Facts!'

The speaker, and the schoolmaster, and the third grown person present, all backed a little, and swept with their eyes the inclined plane of little vessels then and there arranged in order, ready to have imperial gallons of facts poured into them until they were full to the brim.

On first reading this we may well think it rather amusing, if at times sinister, particularly in the portrayal of the little vessels ready to have imperial gallons of facts poured into them. Nor will we be altogether clear what is going on. Who the speaker is and what right he has to be there making these remarks is not yet clear. And strange things seem to happen to him in the second paragraph. His forefinger seems to take on a life of its own; his forehead, described as a wall with the eyes for a base seems to assume the air of a building, perhaps even becoming confused with the room in which he is speaking. The voice and the hair have an almost disembodied activity. By the end we are attending only to the physical and the unpleasant aspects of the speaker, his knobbly head, the unyielding squareness of his coat, legs and shoulders. Even the pupils, the subject of his discourse, are reduced to vessels. This is in its way significant, though we are not fully to know this until we have read more of the novel: the absence of people from the scene can be taken as an image of the dehumanising effect of the factual education proposed.

When we come back from the novel with certain intuitions the passage gains the power to crystallise and add to our insights. The speaker here is one Thomas Gradgrind, manufac- turer, of the northern industrial town of Coketown, where the ethic is all one of utility to the exclusion of the imagination, the emotions and the spirit. Gradgrind has two children into whom he tries to inculcate his beliefs: one, Tom, becomes a thief and betrayer of his sister; the other, Louisa, accepts a loveless marriage with a coarse banker called Bounderby and then becomes almost fatally involved with a louche dandy of no ideals, Harthouse. Resistant to Gradgrind's methods throughout is Cissy Jupe, child from a travelling circus. We also follow the wretched fortunes of a factory worker Stephen Blackpool, unable to escape from a failed marriage and finally driven from his work and from the town. We return from the narrative full of a sense of the disastrous results of an education that rests entirely on facts, of a factory system that reduces people to ciphers and of a social system that refuses help or compassion to the unfortunate. Looking then once more at this passage, what do we see? In comparison to much of what follows it has an aspect of grotesque exaggeration: and if we ask why, we may guess both from this and from its prominence in the novel that it is intended to operate symbolically. Certainly there is enough hint of this from the ironies within which it is framed. The general title given to the first part of the novel which this opens is 'SOWING': the agricultural and natural associations of this seem reversed, to say the least, when we find that what is to be 'planted' are hard facts, not growing but fixed things; and they are to be planted not in receptive soil but in a context where living people have been turned to dead vessels. Certainly the contrast between the natural and the unnatural is one that comes over strongly here. And we may also be driven to reflect on the setting of almost the entire novel in a dark town: no countryside here, little truly wild life, only people shut in, shut in by facts, shut in by factories (the pun is half-meant here), shut inside dead relationships. And then there is the title to this chapter, 'The One Thing Needful': we may feel the biblical reference, but at any rate we will sense that the one thing that is truly needful for humanity and education is not what is described here. The title poses the need for spiritual things that the content of the chapter obstinately ignores – and, we may reflect, that almost everything about Coketown described in the book ignores.

So what now of the passage itself? We do not see the speaker. He is not introduced to us, and we hear him only as a voice. In the second paragraph he is reduced to a series of gestures, themselves lost by links with walls or plantations. In the same way, we find, we do not really see the schoolmaster, only his gown. We hear about a third 'grown' (the word seems ironic) person present: this 'person' is given no sex or identity. The pupils, and we have to deduce it is they, are described only as an 'inclined plane of little vessels'. This we could just link to a theme of dehumanising that runs through the novel. People and their true needs are lost. Later we have a picture of Coketown which shows how the 'hands' – and that is all they are – are crushed by their surroundings. And people behave inhumanly throughout, unable to relate truly, or even when they want to, prevented from doing so. Tom thinks only of himself; Louisa thinks nothing of herself; Blackpool's workmates reject him and he is bound to a loveless marriage. All are isolated.

But the picture of the speaker in the passage goes much further than this. If we let our minds play over it for a time, we may see that each of the sentences in that second paragraph describes some separate part of the speaker's anatomy or clothing. We hear of the action of his forefinger; then how his emphasis is further helped by the square wall of his forehead, the dark caves of his eyes, his inflexible voice, his hair, his legs, his coat, his shoulders, his neckcloth. Indeed each of them takes on a certain amount of life of its own. The forehead and the eyebrows seem to make for themselves a wall and its base while the eyes secrete themselves in two dark caves. The voice seems inflexible and dictatorial on its own initiative. The hair waves and bristles by itself on the head. The head seems forced out into protuberances by the hard facts inside it. The carriage, coat, legs and shoulders by now all separately seem to move and have life. Finally the neckcloth actually seems to take him by the throat rather than being tied by him about it. The speaker seems to be seen as an amalgam of 'bits'.

In what way might this be appropriate in the novel as a whole? It can, if we push the point, serve to highlight several aspects. If we think of the way society is portrayed in the novel, it is as an assemblage of pieces, not as a living unity. Without a soul, without a true self, one's identity becomes fragmented. And if we think of what is being proposed here in this passage, the inculcation of facts, we may question its purpose. Is it done out of any philosophic belief or understanding of the way society should be run? No rationale is given for it here: facts are to be taught, and that is all there is to it. Left without any central reason, except some blind empiricism, for the pursuit of these facts, the consequences so far as education is concerned are manifest a little later in the definition given by one of the pupils, appropriately named Bitzer, of a horse: ' "Quadruped. Graminivorous. Forty teeth, namely twenty-four grinders, four eye-teeth and twelve incisive. Sheds coat in the spring; in marshy countries, sheds hoofs, too. Hoofs hard, but requiring to be shod with iron. Age known by marks in mouth". Thus (and much more) Bitzer'. This is just a collection of facts and pieces. We do not see the horse, only some of its attributes. There is no sense of unity in the picture, no notion of a living and individual animal. The teaching of facts is the teaching of unrelated facts. And this is one version of the other unrelations that we can find running through the novel.

More than this, the teaching of facts without reason or soul behind it produces a domination of material things over things of the spirit: and this we can see in the passage in the way not only that the speaker has become himself a mass of material facts like the horse that Bitzer is later to describe, but in the way that the life the man has refused for himself goes into those very material things, so that they take on an existence of their own while his identity is obscured (hence the mere 'speaker'). The speaker's continual prescription of 'nothing but Facts', 'Plant nothing else and root out everything else', 'nothing else', suggests the reductiveness of the process: this education will not add but take away. Seen from this position, even the fragmentary narrative of the novel, the plot covering Stephen Blackpool having little to do with the lives of the Gradgrinds, Tom living his existence and Louisa hers, all told in separate chapters, becomes significant.

It is not that this passage alone has the power to open up the novel in this way. Rather we bring back to it our experience of the novel, and the beginnings of our own intuitions as to its themes and connections: whereupon, partly through analysis on its own, and partly by seeing the passage in the light of those intuitions, our ideas become much more clearly formulated, and at the same time we see much more. The fragmentary nature of the passage may make us think of the fragmentary nature of the education it describes, the fragmentary nature of the novel itself and the final isolation of the people with it. The absence of humanity in the passage, and the materialism of the description may make us think further of the absence of emotion and spirit in the novel. The unnaturalness that is emphasised here can lead us to the unnatural development of Gradgrind's children, the 'unnaturalness' that Stephen Blackpool is to talk about in the system. The monotony of the description in the passage, 'The emphasis was helped . . . .' not only gives a sense of the facts being driven in like nails, or of the hideous monotony of the scene, or of impersonality in the sentence constantly being started not with a person but with a dead quality and a passive verb: but of the reductiveness of this mania for facts, whereby true facts become invisible and a man is so fixed in his views that he knows nothing whatever of the real natures and needs of his children, his wife, his hired men. Seen thus or similarly this passage can help to give more organic unity to the novel than we might otherwise have perceived.

5
Making
Connections

The business of making connections is one quite simply of taking all or as many as possible of the separate details of a text and discovering some common feature in them. In practice what often happens is that the process of putting one thing beside another yields an idea which can be tested against the rest. At some point, as with all criticism, this involves a measure of imposition of the idea on the material, and the truest interpretation will be that to which the text answers with least forcing. This process of making connections is really that of most critical interpretation: the examples given here will show only one or two of the myriad ways in which it can be done. The main thing, as with every other process in this book, is that the activity should be a pleasure and the mind ceaselessly exploratory.

Suppose we are looking at Chaucer's *The Miller's Tale*. The story is as follows. A clerk, Nicholas, boards in a carpenter's house and he and the carpenter's wife, Alison, look for an opportunity to go to bed together. At the same time the parish clerk, Absolon, attempts in vain to woo Alison himself. Nicholas pretends to have been granted a vision, which the superstitious carpenter, John, is brought readily to believe, that there will soon be a second flood and that the only way to prepare for it is secretly to make ready three large wooden tubs, provisioned, and to hang them in the rafters of the main room of his house. When the flood is imminent, he, Nicholas and Alison will climb into the tubs, and when the water rises they will cut the retaining ropes, break through the roof and float away to freedom. On the night before the supposed flood all three thus stow themselves: and when they are sure that John is asleep, Nicholas and Alison climb down from their

66 CRITICAL THINKING

boats to the carpenter's bed below. Towards dawn, Absolon
comes in hope of wooing Alison by playing and singing below
her window. To remove him Alison offers him a kiss, but
instead of her mouth gives him in the pitch darkness through
the window her posterior. Furious, Absolon goes and borrows
a red-hot coulter from the blacksmith, returns, and pretends
he has a gift for Alison. This time Nicholas resolves to play
Alison's trick, adding a fart for good measure: he is then
branded on his rear so painfully that his screams wake the
carpenter, who, thinking that the flood has indeed come, cuts
the ropes of his boat, falls to the ground and breaks his arm.
When the villagers gather at the noise, Nicholas and Alison
describe the flood-scheme as though it were the carpenter's
idea, and thus make him the laughing-stock of the village.

We can start from any aspect of the tale, trying to find a
hint that will open out the story. As so often, we will start
from what seems to stick out – an odd image, a peculiar plot
device, even a strange turn of phrase. Here for instance the
idea of the second flood and the boats is striking. It is an
extraordinary scheme through which to engineer a piece of
mere cuckoldry. It is made more striking, if we think about
it, by the fact that in a sense, apart from the comedy to be
derived from it, it was unnecessary: John the carpenter was
away from home, and overnight, often enough for Nicholas
and Alison to have slept together. Why then we may ask did
Nicholas use *this* scheme? Of course, we can say that from the
point of view of the narrator, the carpenter's readiness to
believe in the notion of a second flood is meant to show
his ignorance, since God is shown in the Bible specifically
promising that there will be no second flood. But still, *why* a
flood? Much acquaintance with and thought about the text
will probably be necessary before we can proceed further and
begin to make connections. But, this granted, maybe our
minds play about the image of those boats in the rafters of
the room and then John, Nicholas and Alison concealed in
them. Then, thinking about such enclosure in a room, it could
just occur to us that much of the action of the tale takes place
inside a house. Not only that, much of the tale is founded on
rooms or enclosures. Inside the tubs, each person is in a
separate enclosure. But outside is still another enclosure – the
room, in the rafters of which they are hung. But then when

the flood comes they will leave all enclosures, for the boats will float free and they will break out of the house through the roof. Yet in a sense even then they will still not be exposed, because all the rest of the world will be dead – it will simply be a larger version of the private room or 'enclosure' they have just left. Then we can think of another room mentioned in the tale. To awaken the carpenter's interest, Nicholas lies on his bed in his locked room feigning a trance, and to get to him the carpenter has to have the door broken down; then, thinking that Nicholas is possessed by wicked spirits, John sets about putting a spell on the door and the four walls of the house, to banish them and make a safe enclosure. And over all as said there is the whole context of the house in which everything in the tale takes place.

If we have got this far, our minds may now move towards the analogous notion of mental enclosures. It is a standard process: once a concept works clearly in one area it is likely to be found to work in others. The house can be seen as in a sense an image of Alison's enclosure by her much older and jealous husband, who keeps her 'narwe in cage'. Then the carpenter himself is enclosed in his own ignorance and supersitition: because he is like this, he cannot see out to what is really going on. Further, turning the image back again, his ignorance can be seen as expressed in the tub to which he keeps while the other two emerge from theirs and come together; equally his keeping to the rafters can be seen as figuring his being cut off from reality. Now we may think again of another enclosure in the tale: Nicholas's room, into which the carpenter has to break. This room may be said to be like the 'secret' into which Nicholas then admits him. But the secret that Nicholas exposes to him is a lie: there is a further hidden mental chamber behind the one that the carpenter now believes to have been revealed to him. What we have here is a scheme within a scheme, a kind of Chinese box motif. And we can find this reflected in the plot as a whole, where each item, apparently self-enclosed, triggers off the other, as Absolon, in branding Nicholas, makes him call for water, which in turn makes the carpenter think he means the flood has come, and cut himself down. And till the end of the tale Nicholas and Alison live in a mental enclosure of scheming.

How far is that enclosure ever broken into? At the end it is
the carpenter who is exposed to the populace, not Nicholas
and Alison: though certainly, unless she had the craft of May
in *The Merchant's Tale*, who managed to convince her husband
against the evidence of his own senses that she had not been
copulating with the squire Damian, Alison's dealings with
Nicholas would have been revealed to her husband through
his accident. Perhaps now we may think of the other exposure
in the tale, which fits in with the rest and makes the whole
begin to seem coherent – the tricks played on Absolon. Both
Nicholas and Alison stick their most private ('enclosed') parts
out not only from their clothes but from the house window
into the street, though they are still visually enclosed by
darkness. And, thinking of that word 'private', we may well
notice how often it is used throughout the tale, in a whole
range of contexts. Nicholas is 'sleigh and ful privee', he catches
Alison 'prively by the queynte', Alison warns him to be 'privee'
in his plans, he pretends to know God's 'pryvetee', he
persuades John to set up the tub-boat 'in pryvetee' from the
outside world, John tells his 'pryvetee' to his wife, Absolon
comes 'pryvely' to the window, Nicholas puts out his posterior
'pryvely'.

By now the polarity of enclosure/exposure or private/public
is proving a useful intellectual spanner for this tale: without
much forcing the whole work is answering to it. What then of
the characters themselves: suppose we ask what they have to
do with this theme? It may then occur to us that Nicholas
stays in the house throughout, while Absolon remains outside –
fitting image perhaps of the fact that Absolon never gets
'inside' Alison as Nicholas does. Can we follow these contrasts
up in the peculiarly detailed character-portraits we are given
in the tale – those of Nicholas, Alison and Absolon? This, for
instance, is a sample of the portrait of 'hende Nicholas':

> Of deerne love he koude and of solas;
> And therto he was sleigh and ful privee,
> And lyk a mayden meke for to see.
> A chambre hadde he in that hostelrye
> Allone, withouten any compaignye,
> Ful fetisly ydight with herbes swoote;

> And he hymself as sweete as is the roote
> Of lycorys, or any cetewale.
>
> (ll. 3200–7)

Nicholas is certainly a secretive or 'enclosed' person: he can sing of secret or 'deerne' love; he looks as meek as a maiden; though he lives alone in his room, the fact that he keeps himself and the place perfumed with spices suggests his being ready for any female visitor. People come from outside to find out from him what will happen in the future, for his craft is that of an astrologer. His learning seems detached from worldly concerns, being knowledge of the secrets of the heavens; and he is poor (ll. 3190–8). The carpenter thinks of him as being so cut off from earthly matters that he might easily suffer a fate similar to that of the clerk who fell into a marl-pit from too much studying of the stars (ll. 3457–61): but the real Nicholas is 'enclosed' from his learning, and much more worldly than it might imply. In contrast to the clerk described in the General Prologue to *The Canterbury Tales*, he treats the instruments of his knowledge as mere apparatus, which does not expose or act as a sign of his true nature: these instruments come after the perfumes of his room, with which they rhyme:

> Of lycorys, or any cetewale.
> His Almageste, and bookes grete and smale,
> His astrelabie, longynge for his art,
> His augrym stones layen faire apart,
> On shelves couched at his beddes heed. . . .
>
> (ll. 3207–11)

Nicholas' enclosure is only apparent, a means to an end, not an index to his character. Though he seems cut off from reality, he has a firm grasp on it: indeed his first act in the tale is to grasp it literally, in the most direct manner, as he seizes Alison by the 'queynte'.

At this stage of our investigation we are quite simply *looking* for evidence of the enclosure/exposure motif in the tale. We have committed ourselves to an approach which is necessarily narrowing what we notice: but if what we have found is substantially present, this is a price we are prepared to pay for the time. Thus too with Alison. Unlike Nicholas, Alison is described as leaving the house, when she goes to church and Absolon becomes besotted with her (ll. 3307–9, 3339ff.). Her husband keeps her 'narwe in cage', and this goes against her 'wilde and yong' nature: she is ready to break out at any opportunity. Again we observe that, unlike Nicholas, her nature is obvious to all beholders, is 'exposed', not hidden: 'sikerly she hadde a likerous ye', 'She was a prymerole, a piggesnye,/For any lord to leggen in his bedde,/Or yet for any good yeman to wedde' (ll. 3244, 3268–70). We may recall that nothing was said of Nicholas's apearance: but the whole description of Alison is in terms of her appearance – her clothes, her body, her eyebrows, her sweet mouth, her stature. There is no specific mention of her character, but it could be said that her spirit shines through her, and that she seems as natural as the creatures, blossoms, flowers and fruits with which she is constantly compared – weasel, pear-tree, wool, swallow, kid, calf, apples, primrose, 'pig's eye' flower (trillium).

And there are other evidences of her 'public' or 'exposed' nature we can find. Throughout the account of her we may notice that there is a sense of the appraising public view: 'She was ful moore blisful on to see / Than is the newe pere-jonette tree'; 'In al this world, to seken up and doun, / There nys no man so wys that koude thenche/So gay a popelote or swich a wenche'. Then we may remark how she is described as appealing to every sense: she is 'softer than the wolle is of a wether', she sings like a swallow, her mouth is as 'sweete as bragot or the meeth,/Or hoord of apples leyd in hey or heeth'; her feel, smell and almost taste could be said to bring the reader, and others, very close to her. Then we think of how she seems to have more clothes on, and more notice is taken of them, than with almost any other of Chaucer's female characters; yet this can be seen as only a way of heightening the sense of what she would be like with them off: indeed the description of her starts with mention of her body,

> Faire was this yonge wyf, and therwithal
> As any wezele hir body gent and smal.
> A ceynt she werede, barred al of silk,
> A barmcloth eek as whit as morne milk

Upon her lendes, ful of many a goore.
Whit was her smok, and broyden al bifoore
And eek bihynde, on her coler aboute,
Of col-blak silk, withinne and eek withoute.

(ll. 3233–40)

For Alison, exposure is not really an issue, for there is nothing of herself that she would, finally, hide. What she is and what she appears, her 'enclosed' and 'exposed' selves, are basically the same.

And Absolon? He too can be shown to fit readily into the pattern. He is like Nicholas in that he is artful, but there the comparison stops: Absolon's art is aimed at exposure, at making himself appear to others what he thinks he is, a gay courtly lover: his misfortune is that he fails, and that the appearance he presents rather exposes the absurd reality of what he is. Then, where Alison is a cynosure and people come to Nicholas, we see Absolon continually going out to the world, casting his eyes over the wives of the parish, dancing and singing to the barmaids of every ale house in the town, or 'with compaignye, hym to disporte and playe' (ll. 3660). Again, where Nicholas sings to amuse himself, Absolon sings to attract women. And where Nicholas has one occupation, Absolon has several – he is not only parish clerk but hair-dresser, legal clerk, and, since the last is linked by rhyme to his dancing, dancer no less than the others (ll. 3327–8). He is a creature, we may say, wholly of the public world. And he is all appearance and no substance. He may like to try to look like a courtly lover, but the picture of him pestering the women of the village with his simpering advances, or capering and singing in a high treble to his 'smal rubible', or being 'somdeel squaymous / Of fartyng' (l. 3328ff.), suggests an effeminate nature incapable of real physical love; even his name is effeminate, sounding as it does like 'Alison'.

At this point we have materials sufficient to draw the tale together, to make a pattern of significance out of the motif we have found. How might this run? We could say that the moral suggested by the story is clearly some fusion of 'enclosure' and 'exposure', private and public. John and Absolon are in their different ways too enclosed in their delusions: their schemes come to nothing because unlike Nicholas and Alison they are not in touch with reality. At the same time John and Absolon are the two poles of 'enclosure' and 'exposure', in the sense that John ends in complete enclosure in a room within a room, where Absolon is all 'outside' and can only exist outside the house in the public world. And then we could draw in the oddity of the plot, whereby the elaborate scheme of the flood was quite unnecessary if copulation were all that Nicholas and Alison wanted. We could argue – it is a *little* tenuous – that they did not want sex simply, but sex which came as close as possible to disaster, and also a situation which was extremely comic. To that extent they could be said to be 'detached' from sex – or, to put it another way, to be not so 'enclosed' in it that they exclude other modes of experience from it. And, going on, we could say that they wanted to court exposure: they did not want to be comfortably enclosed in the sexual act, but to risk discovery by an outside world. In short, we could argue that in their enjoyment of sex they unite the categories of enclosure and exposure which are otherwise divorced in the tale. And in the light of that norm we could make sense of the branding of Nicholas at the end by saying that it is the consequence of his having lost his sense of balance and gone too far towards 'exposure' in trying to repeat Alison's trick.

But all this may seem rather too conceptual and narrowing, even if the fact that the motif seems quite strongly present in the tale invites it. Its presence here is simply to show the end point of a critical procedure that has started from a hint and worked outwards. And we can – in Chaucer's case at least — go even further outwards than this, to find the motif present in others of his works. For instance, in *Troilus and Criseyde* it can be argued that much of the weakness of the love of Troilus and Criseyde – if also its magnificence – springs from the fact that the lovers exist in an enclosed world, totally cut off from Troy, from the war, and even from time and space. And in *The Parliament of Fowls*, the poem moves between two poles, the rejectionist, 'outside' view of love and life figured in Scipio's Olympian dream, and the claustrophobic over-valuation of love from inside, imaged in the temple of Venus.

Suppose now we try actually to recreate the experience whereby one finds a clue that opens up a text. (No assumption, of course, is being made that the particular direction followed here will be that of any other reader.) As example take *Paradise Lost*. Let us suppose that we have sat over the poem and that we are faced with such hoary topics as, 'Is Satan the hero of the poem?', 'Is God unpleasant?', 'Are Adam and Eve fallen before they fall?' and so forth, and we are embarking at best on an analysis of how far Satan's eminence in Hell is continually deflated from within his speeches, or how far it was necessary that God should speak as he does in Book III, or whether Eve's leaving Adam despite his warnings in Book IX was an act of independence finally sanctioned within the cosmic scheme: and suddenly we are perhaps feeling how much of a game it all is, and how familiar the track we are following, whether for or against, for it has all been canvassed a thousand times before. Our minds perhaps drift – of course this scene is conjectural: we think how intellectual and legalistic much of this debate is, even if it is to some extent matched by a similar character in the poem; we consider how after all the whole poem is the retelling of a story, and in the startling and striking imagery of a pictured cosmos; we let our minds move among Milton's planets and sun, his Heaven, Earth and Hell. What are they there for? Of course, they in a sense have to be, because Milton is telling the story of how Satan was cast out of Heaven to Hell, how the universe was created by God: distance and space matter in theological terms, for evil is divorced from good. Yet the whole situation produces that marvellously-described epic journey of Satan's, up from Hell, past its adamantine gates, through the tumult of Chaos and out into clear space, with the Empyrean beyond, and far off, hanging from it by a golden chain, the Earth, or rather the nine concentric crystalline spheres of which the Earth can form the centre (Book II, 1046–53). That picture of the world is suggestive, and if the mind dwells on it to bring the suggestion out, we may find that what we have before us is an image of an ovum hanging from a womb. Forget for the moment that science in Milton's day, before the application of microscopes, did not know of such things. The image strikes, it may seem no more than locally significant, yet our imaginations are excited by the account of the journey, an account which has little to do with the theology of the poem, except perhaps to demonstrate the tenacity of evil and increase our sense of horror; and now maybe our minds look down from Satan's vantage point, walking like a vulture over the outermost of the crystalline spheres, before discovering that a single passage leads all the way down through the spheres, to Earth (III. 418–43, 526–43). And now Satan hurls himself in flight down that aerial passage, and with that our minds might just possibly begin to formulate the notion that what is being described here is, so far as the imagery goes, rather like an act of fertilisation.

As yet this would be only tentative, a mere curious thought; but then we may look back to Hell and consider how Satan's journey is first through the concave of Hell, before he with difficulty passes through the resistant gateway into the vast abrupt of Chaos, where he is battered to and fro by titanic minds, and how he is described as if a microbe as he 'With head, hands, wings or feet pursues his way,/And swims or sinks, or wades, or creeps, or flies' (II. 949–50); and as we do so the suggestion of a spermatozoon making its dangerous journey to its goal could begin to be more clearly present. We notice too that Satan is one from a myriad. Then, looking forward, we see him enter Paradise, which again is a place with only one gate to it. We may find, too, that the description of Paradise suggests the female genitals (a suggestion, our scholarly edition of the poem will tell us, which is commonly present in accounts of Paradise):

> delicious Paradise,
> Now nearer, crowns with her enclosure green,
> As with a rural mound the champaign head
> Of a steep wilderness, whose hairy sides
> With thicket overgrown, grotesque and wild
> Access denied.
>
> (IV. 132–7)

By now we are beginning to fit the whole poem into the scheme. This is the stage of excitement at seeing how things fit; it is also the stage at which in our headlong career we ignore and minimise those things that do not fit: such is the stuff of all interpretation.

The fecund interior of Paradise can be seen, too, as a womb – 'a circling row/Of goodliest trees loaden with fairest fruit,/Blossoms and fruits at once of golden hue/

Appeared' (ll. 146–9); it is a small protected place, 'In narrow room nature's whole wealth, yea more' (l. 207). Satan first enters by leaping over the wall, and perhaps this may be one reason for his failure. His next attempt is more 'natural' in that he enters by the river that goes under the hill of Paradise and comes up as a fountain in the middle to water the garden; and again the notion of the fountain and its irrigation is a resonant image. But most striking of all, suddenly adding new validity to all this speculation, is the fact that the form which Satan assumes in order to tempt Eve is that of the serpent, the express image of the spermatozoon. (He is unsuccessful in his first disguise as a toad.) His temptation of her is described in terms which suggest seduction. The image of him as a city dweller taking a day trip to the country underlines this:

> If chance with nymph-like step fair virgin pass,
> What pleasing seemed, for her now pleases
> > more,
> She most, and in her look sums all delight.
> Such pleasure took the serpent to behold
> This flowery plat, the sweet recess of Eve
> Thus early, thus alone; her heavenly form
> Angelic, but more soft, and feminine . . . .
> > (IX. 452–8)

So now we start looking for seduction images elsewhere. And that we appear to be on something like the right track is suggested by the fact that we readily find them. Earlier, in his seductive speech to Eve in her induced dream (V. 38–48), Satan said, 'with ravishment/Attracted by thy beauty still to gaze./I rose . . . .' (ll. 46–8). Eve herself is compared to the pursued virgins Pales, Pomona and Ceres (IX. 393–6). Satan's serpentine shape, we are told, is lovely and alluring (IX. 503–5); he approaches Eve with 'tract oblique', like a ship tacking about before entering the mouth of a river (ll. 513–16); he 'Curled many a wanton wreath in sight of Eve,/To lure her eye' (ll. 517–18) and 'Fawning . . . licked the ground whereon she trod' (l. 526). Satan is 'erect / Amidst his circling spires' (ll. 501–2); later, 'He bolder now, uncalled before her stood' (l. 523); and, before his final temptation speech, he 'Fluctuates disturbed, yet comely, and in act/Raised, as of some great matter to begin' (ll. 668–9). His speech itself, we might even say, is not so much an argument as a rhetorical rape. His words are described as penetrating her: 'Into the heart of Eve his words made way' (l. 550); and, when she is persuaded to eat of the Tree, 'his words replete with guile/Into her heart too easy entrance won' (ll. 733–4). Frequently in the poem man is directly described as having been 'seduced' by Satan (i. 219; ii. 368; vi. 901; ix. 287, 901; x. 41, 332, 485, 577); even allowing for the Latinate sense of the word, 'lead away', the other meaning is also present. In a sense therefore we can say that Hell or evil has fertilised mankind with itself. But then what further sense can be made of this in the whole cosmic scheme? Our minds may perhaps move to the consequences of all this, the Christ who will be the Second Adam. And then suddenly we may happen on the insight that Christ will be born of woman, through the male agency of God – in other words, that God will fertilise man with himself just as Satan did. (We may recall that in John, 3.14 Christ himself is described as a serpent.) God will 'have to' carry out the same essential action as Satan to reply to him.

By now we have a pattern which may make some sense of the large imagery of *Paradise Lost*. But what can we do with it, assuming we have got to this point? It makes an interesting analogy, perhaps, but no more than that: it does not seem to affect our understanding of the poem. Further, we must doubt whether to put the whole in terms of fertilisation does historical justice to the poem. There was in fact in Milton's day no knowledge of spermatozoa or of their journey, mode of travel or method of union. Faced by this, we either have to credit Milton with remarkable prevision, or else look elsewhere for explanation.

When one is up against the 'this-ness' of a work in this way, it is worth turning to the sorts of book that deal in explanations of strange (and recurrent) images in human experience: the serpent/spermatozoon, after all, was not Milton's invention but is there in the beginning, in Genesis. (At this point it should be said that the interpretation that follows here is one which would not readily occur to most readers.) If we were to look through the works of the psychiatrist C. G. Jung, which deal with such images, we might eventually come across certain extraordinary pictures and accounts of mandalas, in the concluding essays of his well-known *The Archetypes and the Collective Unconscious* (tr. 1959). Mandalas are archetypal images, that is, recurrent from the beginnings of mankind and possessed of meanings which transcend the local or merely individual. They are circular in form: the image is frequently a dynamic one in that a serpent figure is associated with it, penetrating the circle and fusing with its contents, which thereupon often divide into four segments, still bound within the sphere. For Jung this fusion of the serpent figure with the circle, and the subsequent fourness, is an archetypal image of psychic or cosmic wholeness and completion. In this image are subsumed the facts of fertilisation, the approach of the spermatozoon to the egg and the subsequent fusion and cellular subdivision: the biological facts are part of a larger imagery applicable to every level of being, physical and mental, individual and social, local and universal. The mandala archetype images the process of fertilisation long before that process is known to man consciously through science and observation. In this sense it will now therefore be possible to make a transference from the terminology of fertilisation in describing the effect of Milton's imagery, to that of the mandala.

By making this transference we will be able to find striking significance in the image, rather than be forced to leave it as an interesting and suggestive pattern. For if as Jung says the mandala archetype, particularly as penetrated by the serpent, is a symbol of psychic wholeness, then it follows that as far as the deepest levels of the poem are concerned, Satan is shown to be essential to the continued health of the universe. And this notion of the serpent or the shadow as the dark side of the self with which the rest of the mind must be integrated is recurrent in the archetypal images described throughout Jung's work.

Having got thus far we may feel that this is enough, since it obviously runs so counter to the official morality of the poem, wherein Satan is anathema or nonentity. And doubtless there will be many critics to say that we have done more than enough to make nonsense of the poem. But our business is not to say the 'right' thing about a work, but fairly to trace patterns in it and see where they naturally can lead us. That they here take us into strange yet not, on this reading, chimerical realms, may suffice to show how dramatically the simple technique of making connections can expand and transform our views of texts.

And so in the determination of connections, one can start with such crucial images as the fog in Dickens's *Bleak House*, the river in Conrad's *Heart of Darkness*, the Marabar Caves in Forster's *A Passage to India*, the cliff in Shakespeare's *King Lear*, the castle of Gormenghast in Mervyn Peake's *Titus Groan*, the lighthouse in Virginia Woolf's *To the Lighthouse*. With most of them however it is a case of trying to integrate the image with what we already know about the text, and finding out more in the process. But this is far from the only technique of establishing connections in a work. We saw with *The Miller's Tale* that another was detecting similarities of situation or recurrences of a motif – there of rooms or interiors, or of privacy. For instance, in trying to make connections apart from the narrative ones with Dickens's *Great Expectations*, we might note that one of the most frequent feelings the hero Pip has throughout the novel is one of guilt: guilt at having helped a convict, guilt at being low-born before his beloved Estella, guilt or shame at being seen with the convict, guilt at having been proud when he came into money and rejecting or patronising his old friends. Having noticed this motif, and perhaps the concomitant one of Pip's constantly being physically uncomfortable or else emotionally ill at ease throughout the novel, we then try to find some explanation for it. The main thing though is to see the likenesses in so many different episodes in the first place. By this means we bring together such diverse moments as Pip's sensations after having hidden the bread and butter for the convict down his trouser leg, his awkwardness at suddenly being asked to 'play' by the strange Miss Havisham, his clumsy jealousy at the favour in which the rough Bentley Drummle is held both by his financial guardian Mr Jaggers and his beloved Estella, or his sensations as the convicts breathe down his neck on the stagecoach back home.

But there are other methods of tracing connections which will apply with different sorts of work. For instance, where we have an (auto)biographical narrative, or indeed any narrative of process, it will be for us to trace not only the stages of the

development but to characterise it. Consider as example James
Joyce's *A Portrait of the Artist as a Young Man*. This describes
the growth from childhood of one Stephen Dedalus in Dublin,
to the point where he resolves to quit his country because it
is too confining for his spirit. The story may be traced simply
at a narrative level. Stephen has a happy early childhood,
though he is eventually sent to the rigours of a well-to-do
Jesuit school. His father's fortunes decline and Stephen is
faced too with reduced expectations. Developing sexually, he
consorts with prostitutes; but then after hearing a terrifying
series of sermons at school on the nature of Hell and the
terrible afflictions loaded on sinners, he desperately repents
and tries to transform his life. He trains to be a priest, but
at last the life or rather apparent death-in-life of a father
confessor revolts him, and he leaves the novitiate. After that
he enters university and reads literature. It is while he is there
that he realises that his soul will die if he does not leave
Ireland, and by the end of the story he is ready to take ship
abroad.

If we look for a pattern in this story, putting its diverse
elements together, we could find it in a series of rebellions. At
school Stephen is singular in being courageous enough to
complain at an unjust beating he has received from a prefect.
He at first refuses to appear in a school play in which he has
a part. Later, having for the time submitted to its sway, he
rebels against the Church, and leaves it. In this he refuses his
mother's dearest wish, that he become a member of the
priesthood. His last action in the book is to crystallise his
growing rebellion against life in Ireland as a whole by leaving
his country. We could say that the scope of his rebellions gets
wider as he himself grows. All these are none-too-surprising
connections, given that Stephen is portrayed throughout as
fundamentally an explorer. We can see this exploring habit
in the smallest as in the largest contexts:

> Was it right to kiss his mother or wrong to kiss his mother? What did
> that mean, to kiss? You put your face up like that to say good night and
> then his mother put her face down. That was to kiss. His mother put
> her lips on his cheek; her lips were soft and they wetted his cheek; and
> they made a tiny little noise: kiss. Why did people do that with their
> two faces?

Or,

> 'Welcome, O life! I go to encounter for the millionth time the reality of
> experience and to forge in the smithy of my soul the uncreated conscience
> of my race'.

Having got this far, we could then ask ourselves what
the point is of the extraordinarily powerful and apparently
anomalous picture of Hell in the story. Here we will be doing
roughly as with the 'tub-plot' in *The Miller's Tale* or the
landscape of *Paradise Lost*, starting from a peculiarity and
trying to integrate it with the material. If we have an idea of
Stephen's development being one of a series of expansions of
the spirit, a development outwards, then we can readily find
point in the portrayal of Hell. For it is seen in terms of
confinement, of fixity, of exclusion, of utter helplessness. Its
eternity is portrayed as unimaginable. The damned are locked
in it so close as to be unable to move a muscle to try to protect
themselves from its pains. It is a place of darkness and of
utter enclosure. And it is a place in which the greatest pain is
the sense of loss, particularly the sinner's exclusion from God.
All this is the antithesis of Stephen's spirit struggling to be
free, even if for the time he is terrified into submission by it.
It is as though the narrative gathered together in this one
central image, multiplied to grotesque extent, all the repression
and cruelty against which Stephen intermittently struggles
throughout his experience. Once we see that, the narrative
becomes 'organic' in quite a new way: we see that it has secret
patterns of meaning that make the seemingly anomalous
emphasis on Hell become integrated. We understand more
about the work than we did before; we begin to sense its living
depths within and beyond the level of conscious narration.
But still beyond all this lies the question of how Stephen
develops and changes over his early life. By the end of the
story he can seem fairly cold in his rejection of the Church,
his mother, his country, even his friends; and he is often to
be found in a mocking or satiric role. When his friend Cranly
asks him whether he is not afraid of being sent to Hell on the
Day of Judgement he can now reply, ' "What is offered me on
the other hand? . . . An eternity of bliss in the company of
the dean of studies?" ' He pictures the artist as someone finally
disengaged from his work, like God from His creation: ' "The

artist, like the God of the creation, remains within or behind or beyond or above his handiwork, invisible, refined out of existence, indifferent, paring his fingernails"'. Stephen has, we may say, become cooler as the story has proceeded, more detached.

Looking at him in this way, we also find a more intellectual Stephen, one who has put a grid between himself and experience. He becomes a theoriser about life and art, for in Ireland he seems unable to live the one or do the other: he cannot commit himself. If we compare him with the Stephen of the early part of the narrative, that Stephen seemed much more bound up with feelings, with his body, with the world. He was strongly aware of his aunt Dante's different coloured hairbrushes, the cold of bog-water, the sounds of the school refectory, the feel of the cane, the smell of the priest's breath at communion, the touch of a whore. But later he does not seem so concerned with the world about him or even with his body. Almost all he does is mental, and all he sees is translated, as when he thinks of how at various sordid locations on his daily walk through Dublin his mind will turn to different authors of the beautiful and the sublime. We could say that not only does he gradually separate himself from Ireland but also in a sense from himself.

Pushing this view further – and again it will take time and practice to do this – we may see that there are far more concrete objects and surroundings in the first part of the story: we know the dormitory at Clongowes, the festive home at Christmas, or the railway journey with his father, but we do not so immediately know the later setting of the university or of Stephen's Dublin perambulations – though it has to be said that a vision he has of a dried-up priest trying to light a fire is vivid enough. Roughly speaking one might even say that the book gives one part to the more physical side of life, the other to the more mental. And it may occur to us that this is mirrored in the portrayal of Hell itself, for the priest who describes it gives one day to its physical torments and another to its spiritual ones.

That the book has two halves as it were of this sort may then be established by further contrasts: if we look closely we will see that Stephen in the first part is constantly looking back to analyse what he has done or experienced, whether kissing his mother or giving way to sin; whereas in the second

there is no such retrospection, and he looks, where he considers
himself, not to what he has been or done, but to what he may
become: at first concerned with the past, his time-orientation
later shifts to the future. That of course is reasonably natural,
but it does add to the sense of division in the book. And what
can we make of this division? So far as the separation of 'body'
from 'mind' is concerned, we could say it points to an inability
to be a whole man: somehow Stephen's psyche seems split.
Thus the Stephen we have at the end may be a development,
but not necessarily a progess – maybe he has simplified himself
too much in order to leave Ireland, has shut away in his
intellectual fastidiousness much that may return to draw him
back. And this is partly, borne out in *Ulysses*, where we find
him once more returned to Dublin.

Another area of literature in which the determination of
connections is the first objective is in works of some obscurity
or indirection, where one has to try to make sense of them or
leave them unknown. As an example we can take Norman
MacCaig's 'Explorer':

> Trampling new seas with filthy timbers, he
> Jotted down headlands, speculated on
> Vestigial civilizations, ate strange fruits
> And called his officers Mister. When sails were gone
>
> Bundling and tumbling down the shrieking dark,
> He trailed the Bible as sea-anchor; when
> Reefs shaved the barnacles from the keel, he took
> His gentlemanly snuff. Each night at ten,
>
> Under the lamp from which his cabin swung,
> He logged the latest, drank his grog and spread,
> With only one uncomprehending sigh,
> His wild uncharted world upon his bed.
>
> (*A Round of Applause*, 1962)

The poem's title, 'Explorer', here gives us some idea of its
subject – which is far from always the case with the titles of
obscure poems. The context seems reasonably settled: here
we have a sailor charting new seas. But we can see that that
is not all there is to it. The first thing that strikes us is the

sheer number and diversity of the details in the poem. What has 'trampling new seas with filthy timbers' got to do with jotting down headlands, or taking snuff? What does 'He trailed the Bible as sea-anchor' mean? Why are we given 'the lamp from which his cabin swung' rather than 'the lamp which from his cabin swung'? A whole series of acts emanating from this one person, the explorer, is described. Indeed, if we consider our experience of the poem more closely, we may see that it is full of violated expectations. Most of us think of explorers as romantic figures, yet in the first line we are told of this one that he tramples 'new seas with filthy timbers'; then, no sooner have we got the impression of something scruffy and disreputable, than we have the detachment of his coolly jotting down and speculating. Again, no sooner do we become used to the objects of his explorations – 'vestigial civilisations', 'strange fruits' – than the poem suddenly swings back to 'And called his officers Mister', before the abrupt and unfinished 'When sails were gone'. And so we find it through the other two stanzas. The poem seems to keep changing direction. Why might this be? Here we have this explorer . . . . What is he searching for? What is the point of his exploration? Perhaps he himself does not know where he is going. And that would certainly tie in with elements in the last stanza. There we are told how he would spread 'With only one uncomprehending sigh,/His wild uncharted world upon his bed': what this says is that the explorer who seeks to know more of the outer world knows very little of the world within him. Then we might be led to reflect that perhaps his exploration of the outer world and his failure to explore the inner world may be related: going further, maybe he explores the outer world as a way of avoiding exploration of himself.

For the moment this last idea is ambitious; and we had better fill out our impression of the explorer as conveyed by the poem. One of the best ways to do this, given that there are several lists of items in the poem, is to see what some or all of these items may have in common. Certain details may seem to us to belong together. The simplest point at which to start is with him taking snuff while reefs shave the keel. We can see from this the clear implication that he is a cool head in a crisis. More than this, it is a 'gentlemanly' head; and this may link back for us to the way in the first stanza he is

described as calling his officers Mister. Since the taking of the
snuff is described in parallel with the trailing of the Bible as
sea-anchor in storms, we may then suppose that a similar
portrayal of the explorer is implied there. We will notice the
way the use of the Bible is described, as though it were simply
another nautical technique: and this may suggest to us that
the faith the explorer deploys in such moments is no frantic
thing, but as calculated as anything else in his life. We notice
other statements in the poem in parallel with these. 'Each
night at ten / . . . / He logged the latest' is again precise and
well-ordered. 'Jotted down headlands' seems strange, but
most evidently describes the way he simply reduced the outside
world to parts of a map. 'Speculated on/Vestigial civilizations'
again suggests detached inquiry: and perhaps we may feel
that the abstract words here seem to further this impression.

Beyond this we begin to get an impression of someone with
a marked ability to reduce the external world to what
he wants. Headlands become jottings, vestigial civilizations
speculations, officers reduced to manageable Misters; storms
and dangers are dealt with according to set patterns. But one
piece of reality, we have already become aware, this man
cannot subdue: and that is the inner world of himself described
in the last stanza. Other things he can chart, but not this, 'His
wild uncharted world'. When we read that phrase, it reminds
us of the wild uncharted worlds he has been subduing earlier
in the poem, whether in the form of newly-discovered lands,
or in the shape of storms. He too, for all his control over the
wilderness outside, has none over that which lies within. The
man of such rational control has the primitive at his heart.
At this point we have enough data to suggest why, for instance,
in the first line of the last stanza the cabin is described as
though it swung from the lamp: the reversal of expectation
here suggests perhaps the upside-down nature of the explorer's
life.

If we have let the poem speak to us without forcing a
meaning out of it, we will feel, when we understand some of
it in this way, not a sense of having unravelled some needless
code, but rather how the poem could only have said what it
does in the form in which it was written. And by now, perhaps,
other aspects of this form become more evident to us. For
instance, we may feel how the syntax of the last stanza is

much longer and less jerky than in the previous two stanzas.
There we are told of a whole series of actions by the explorer:
here he is preparing himself for sleep. In sleep one lets oneself
go. And the mention of the wild uncharted world reminds us
that sleep is, too, the province of dreams and the unconscious
mind. Impressions we have had of his previous actions begin
to sharpen. Those were most of them deliberate and rational.
Clearly the daylight world could be said to be that of the
conscious mind. Here at night he is shut in for the first time,
in his cabin, and in himself. But it is those verbs that strike
us most: 'he / Jotted', 'speculated', 'ate', 'called', 'trailed',
'took', 'logged', 'drank', 'spread': he has gone out to things,
actively, and subdued them to the limited province of his wit;
but now he is to be passive. There are no verbs, we notice, in
those last two lines: the syntax simply unravels like the mind's
sharp categories melting.

   Much more could doubtless be said. But the point for us here
is the way, faced with that which seemed incomprehensible, we
let its peculiarities work on us until we began to see a way to
make some tentative connections among them; and as these
became established, we moved out to others until the whole
poem began naturally to reveal patterns and significance; and
then these in turn became wedded back into the poem as we
realised some of its underlying movements of style. Doubtless
different works will require different strategies, but on the
whole that of facing the peculiarities of each and trying to
decipher them in relation to others that seem in any way of a
similar character will prove most productive.

6
Comparisons

What use are comparisons? What do we gain by putting one piece of literature beside another like it or different from it? Comparisons can heighten one's sense of the individuality of the writer, his or her special nature, a sense we often lack from gazing too close and without perspective at one alone. If a work translates another, or reworks it, or is heavily dependent on it, then it is often possible to put two versions of the same passage or section together and gain insight into each. And at a wider level we can compare a text with its literary source – as for instance Joyce's *Ulysses* with Homer's *Odyssey*, or Tennyson's *Idylls of a King* with Malory's *Morte d'Arthur* – to see how far the two are alike, and how far not, this again giving insight into the special concerns and themes of each. Or we can compare works of similar form, subject or genre: Shakespeare's use of sonnet with Sidney's or Drayton's, Shakespeare's tragedy *King Lear* with Greek or modern tragedy such as *Oedipus Rex* or *Lord Jim*. We can compare authors that in some ways are unlike to gain a clearer idea of difference – Shakespeare or Donne with Jonson, T.S. Eliot with Swinburne, Pope with Wordsworth. With this last method we can gain a sense of authors or works that almost belong together as paired opposites, as two ways of seeing that together make up a whole.

That shows some of the more deliberate uses to which we can put comparison. But it should be said that it is not just a question of choice in any case. The whole business of analysing literature involves comparisons. We are making comparisons when we trace a recurrent theme through different forms – when, for example, we find that many of the different characters in Dickens's *Bleak House* all suffer from some form of selfishness, from the vain fop Turveydrop to the parasite

Skimpole and from the greasy gluttony of the Reverend
Chadband to the rapacious benevolence of Mrs Pardiggle.
The entire process of making connections in literature, of
seeing how each part contributes to the making of a larger
whole, of building a series of local impressions into a total
view, involves putting one thing beside another.

Here our concern will be with comparisons between different
texts, and the way that their use can give one source of insight
into a work. We can start with an example from Shakespeare's
Antony and Cleopatra. In writing this play Shakespeare was, as
any edition will tell us, using a source, the Roman writer
Plutarch's 'Life of Marcus Antonius' in his *Lives of the Noble
Grecians and Romans*, as translated by Sir Thomas North in
1579. The text of this translation is sometimes reprinted in
editions of *Antony and Cleopatra*, and is certainly readily
available. If we read the play and then the source we will see
how closely Shakespeare has kept to the details of the original,
from mentioning the number of boars supposedly eaten by
Antony and his friends at an Egyptian breakfast, to the details
of Cleopatra's reactions to the news of Antony's marriage or
her dealings with Thyreus and Dolabella, agents of Rome,
and even Seleucus, her treasurer. One scene however sticks
out; it is a passage which has inspired later writers from
Dryden and Pope to T.S. Eliot: the description of how Antony
first met Cleopatra after she came in her barge down the river
Cydnus. The scene will be particularly striking for us here,
however, not because of its inherent nature, but because in
this set-piece Shakespeare follows the translation of Plutarch
line by line as he does not elsewhere. He clearly either had a
word-perfect memory of North's translation, or more likely,
had the book itself open beside him as he wrote. When we
have two passages as closely related as this, it is worth while
examining them to see if they are so alike after all.

In Plutarch's account, Antony's first meeting with Cleopatra
occurs after he has sent to her to demand that she appear
before him to answer certain charges concerning her past
doings on behalf of Brutus and Cassius against Antony.
Encouraged by Antony's messenger, Dellius, Cleopatra resolves to win Antony over by her beauty, and does so first by
delaying and teasing him, and then by choosing her own
method of going to meet him:

... she disdained to set forward otherwise but to take her barge in the
river of Cydnus, the poop whereof was of gold, the sails of purple, and
the oars of silver, which kept stroke in rowing after the sound of the
music of flutes, howboys, citherns, viols, and such other instruments as
they played upon in the barge. And now for the person of herself: she
was laid under a pavilion of cloth of gold of tissue, apparelled and attired
like the goddess Venus commonly drawn in picture; and hard by her,
on either hand of her, pretty fair boys apparelled as painters do set
forth god Cupid, with little fans in their hands, with the which they
fanned wind upon her. Her ladies and gentlewomen also, the fairest of
them were apparelled like the nymphs Nereides (which are the mermaids
of the waters) and like the Graces, some steering the helm, others tending
the tackle and ropes of the barge, out of which there came a wonderful
passing sweet savour of perfumes, that perfumed the wharf's side,
pestered with innumerable multitudes of people. Some of them followed
the barge all alongst the river's side; others also ran out of the city to
see her coming in; so that in the end there ran such multitudes of people
one after another to see her that Antonius was left post-alone in the
market-place in his imperial seat to give audience.

And here is Shakespeare's version, spoken by Antony's lieuten-
ant Enobarbus while talking of Cleopatra in Rome to his
counterpart Agrippa on Caesar's side:

Enobarbus.   The barge she sat in, like a burnish'd throne,
    Burn'd on the water: the poop was beaten gold;
    Purple the sails, and so perfumed that
    The winds were love-sick with them; the oars were silver,
    Which to the tune of flutes kept stroke, and made
    The water which they beat to follow faster,
    As amorous of their strokes. For her own person,
    It beggar'd all description. She did lie
    In her pavilion, cloth-of-gold, of tissue,
    O'erpicturing that Venus where we see
    The fancy out-work nature. On each side her
    Stood pretty dimpled boys, like smiling Cupids,
    With divers-colour'd fans, whose wind did seem
    To glow the delicate cheeks which they did cool,
    And what they undid did.
Agrippa.   O, rare for Antony!
Enobarbus.   Her gentlewomen, like the Nereides,
    So many mermaids, tended her i' th' eyes,
    And made their bends adornings. At the helm
    A seeming mermaid steers. The silken tackle

Swell with the touches of those flower-soft hands,
That yarely frame the office. From the barge
A strange invisible perfume hits the sense
Of the adjacent wharfs. The city cast
Her people out upon her; and Antony,
Enthroned i' th' market-place, did sit alone,
Whistling to th'air; which, but for vacancy,
Had gone to gaze on Cleopatra too,
And made a gap in nature.   (ii.ii.195–222)

The great thing about comparisons such as this is that they
are laid out for us on a plate. We only have to look from one
line to another to see immediate likenesses and differences.
However, while this helps our task considerably, it is still
often difficult to see what are the telling differences: one can
tick off points, but seeing how they build into a larger basic
contrast is another matter. For we may be put off by the mere
fact that the two passages *are* so alike. Shakespeare has
started, like Plutarch, with the barge, gone on to portray its
accoutrements of golden poop and purple sails, described
how the oars kept time to music, and the various musical
instruments, before proceeding to picture Cleopatra herself
and her attendants; then, still following Plutarch, the effect of
the barge on the wharfs, how the people ran out from the city
to see her, and how Antony was left alone in the marketplace.
Faced by such fidelity to the source, why should we feel the
need to differentiate? To that one can answer that the whole
feel of Shakespeare's account is quite other than that of
Plutarch.

We can start by noticing that, however faithful his account,
Shakespeare has put in some things that are not to be found
in Plutarch. He tells us that the sails were so perfumed that
'The winds were love-sick with them', and that the oars which
kept stroke to the tune of flutes made 'The water which they
beat to follow faster, / As amorous of their strokes': Plutarch
has none of this, simply saying that the sails were of purple
and that the rowing kept time to the music played on
the instruments. If we now think about Shakespeare's two
additions, we will see that they are of a similar nature: both
talk about things we would normally consider inanimate, the
wind and the water, behaving as though possessed of human

qualities of love. Near the end of the passage we find another addition: after Shakespeare tells us how Antony was left alone in the marketplace, he portrays him whistling to the air, 'which, but for vacancy, / Had gone to gaze on Cleopatra too, / And made a gap in nature'. Again, we notice, this gives volition to nature: the air would have gone if it could. More than this, all three of these additions increase our sense of the power and admiration evoked by the barge and Cleopatra: she is so wondrous that she has the power to animate the winds and water. And this itself suggests a contrast with Plutarch's more muted account which asks us to look further. (Incidentally, there may be those who wish to trace a pattern of reference to the elements in Shakespeare's version: fire and water in the barge that burns on the water, water made amorous by the barge, the winds (air) become love-sick, the air that would have gone to see Cleopatra if it could.)

It is impossible to tell with what speed and in what direction one's mind will move after noticing such a point, but for the sake of regularity, and perhaps to provide a framework for analysis in such cases, let us proceed to what we may call stage two: the point at which we begin to notice the different ways in which the two writers have presented the same material. Plutarch, as we saw, tells us that Cleopatra was sent for by letters to come to Antony but mocked him and his wishes and took to her barge on the river, in order to win him over on her own terms. Shakespeare's account is, we find, quite different. There is no mention of any prior communication or demand from Antony: all that Enobarbus says is that, 'When she first met Mark Antony she purs'd up his heart, upon the river of Cydnus'. We hear nothing of any motives in her taking to the barge: she is simply set before us in a magnificent image, 'The barge she sat in, like a burnish'd throne, / Burn'd on the water'. She is on the river, Antony is in the city: the encounter seems almost accidental; indeed in a sense is no encounter at all for most of the time, since Antony is left on his own. So that in Shakespeare's account we are left with an element of mystery: we do not know for certain that she has come there, as in Plutarch, to win Antony, or indeed that Cleopatra has any concern with him at all. And this, we may wish to reflect, is what can often be seen in the play itself: we do not know how much Cleopatra truly feels for Antony at almost any time – and he, Roman luxur transformed by the mysterious and ambiguous Egyptian world, often does not know his own feelings.

We notice that in Shakespeare's account we are told that Cleopatra is a wonder. Her own person 'beggar'd all description'; she lies 'O'erpicturing that Venus where we see / The fancy outwork nature', that is, she outdoes something that itself outdoes nature; she is rare for Antony, her nymphs bow before her, the city – itself brought to life by her presence – 'cast[s] / Her people out upon her'. Plutarch, we find however, sees her in less hyperbolic terms, and delivers his description more like a kind of shopping list, a ticking of items: 'And now for the person of herself: she was laid under a pavilion of cloth of gold of tissue, apparelled and attired like the goddess Venus commonly drawn in picture'. Here she is simply one more detail in the scene, on the same level as the coloured sails or the gold poop. 'She was laid' – never mind the unfortunate modern overtones of the phrase, it is still less than happy: it reduces her to dead passivity, an arranged object. Put that beside 'she did lie': we can see that Shakespeare's version has a much more positive air, a sense that she chose to lie. Then that word 'commonly': what unfortunate connotations it lets into the scene! Where in Shakespeare Cleopatra is the non-pareil, in Plutarch she is simply an imitator. And actually in that difference lies all difference. Plutarch's picture is one of artifice, where there is living mystery in Shakespeare. Plutarch leaves one thing merely like another, and often dressed up to look like it, as the 'pretty fair boys apparelled as painters do set forth god Cupid'; but in Shakespeare it is as though the two things being compared partly exchange natures: Cleopatra becomes a sort of Venus, the barge is alive, the boys 'pretty dimpled boys, like smiling Cupids', take on the aspect of the god, participate in his being.

By now we are moving faster and with greater assurance through the comparison. We have gained several impressions of how Plutarch sees Cleopatra in less admiring terms than Shakespeare, and that is helping to guide and sharpen, if sometimes narrow, our response to contrast after contrast in the two passages. And already we are beginning to move from this general sense of difference, this sense that Shakespeare is favourable where Plutarch is not, to a more clearly formulated notion of the difference, one built up in us through our growing experience of the contrasts in the passages. Shakespeare's has Cleopatra as more wondrous, potent enough to make nature itself become voluntary and wish to pay her homage. Plutarch more or less tells us that she arranged the scene to win Antony: Shakespeare leaves matters far more ambiguous. Plutarch makes the whole scene an elaborate artifice, where Shakespeare implies that the barge brought out Cleopatra's true nature, rather than being an attempt to seem more than she was. And in Shakespeare's account that nature is wondrous, semi-divine. With this general impression in mind we can now see other things which remained latent in the passages – for instance the sheer variety of the syntax in Shakespeare's as against the monotonous regularity of the sentence-order in Plutarch. Shakespeare can get life from suspension, as in 'The barge she sat in, like a burnish'd throne, / Burn'd on the water' where the 'Burn'd' comes with full force, and is again heightened by being 'thrown against' the water. Plutarch we find has none of this: Cleopatra took 'to her barge on the river of Cydnus'. Or again we can feel the vigour in 'The poop was beaten gold; / Purple the sails, and so perfumed that / The winds were lovesick with them'. It is partly the poise and swing of the syntax from the poop to the inversion with the sails; partly the alliteration on the 'p' which throws the line into fresh energy and connects one thing with another; and partly again the suspension of the sense over the perfumed sails.

What we see here, more broadly, however, is how our growing sense of the precise nature of the central difference between two passages can lead to a further awareness of other differences we might not immediately have noticed but felt none the less. In comparisons, as observed before, we follow roughly the same procedure that we do in making connections: but in the one we notice differences in apparent similarities, and in the other, similarities in apparent difference. We begin by noticing where exactly the differences come; then we put the separate observations of difference together and begin to have a general or overall impression of whence the difference springs; eventually we come to a point of analysis or interpretation where we can say from what different general standpoint each passage emerges; and after that, armed with this knowledge, we can go back into the passages and find still more contrasts that till now have been latent. Beyond all that, we can move out from the passages themselves to a more general understanding of the differences between the two texts from which they spring. We can say that Shakespeare's Cleopatra is a dangerous wonder, where Plutarch's is a danger; or that Plutarch is at pains to show Cleopatra a calculating seductress where Shakespeare is much more ambiguous throughout his potrayal of her. In this way comparisons work as microcosms: see into a part, and we can begin to see into the whole. And that of course is the method with the comparison itself – we notice the details of differences and then link them up and make sense of them.

Naturally comparisons as close as the one just considered are not often possible. More usually it is a case of comparing works of the same theme or genre. The procedure is the same, but finding where the contrasts come is a little harder. Take as an example two different poems on the subject of death, John Donne's Holy Sonnet X, 'Death be not proud . . . .' and Dylan Thomas's 'And Death Shall Have No Dominion'.

This is Donne's poem:

> Death be not proud, though some have called thee
> Mighty and dreadful, for, thou art not so,
> For, those, whom thou think'st, thou dost overthrow,
> Die not, poor death, nor yet canst thou kill me;
> From rest and sleep, which but thy pictures be,
> Much pleasure, then from thee, much more must flow,
> And soonest our best men with thee do go,
> Rest of their bones, and soul's delivery.
> Thou art slave to fate, chance, kings, and desperate men,
> And dost with poison, war, and sickness dwell,
> And poppy, or charms can make us sleep as well,
> And better than thy stroke; why swell'st thou then?
> One short sleep past, we wake eternally,
> And death shall be no more, Death thou shalt die.

And this is Thomas's:

> And Death shall have no dominion.
> Dead men naked they shall be one

With the man in the wind and the west moon;
When their bones are picked clean and their clean bones
                                                   gone,
They shall have stars at elbow and foot;
Though they go mad they shall be sane,
Though they sink through the sea they shall rise again;
Though lovers be lost love shall not;
And death shall have no dominion.

And death shall have no dominion.
Under the windings of the sea
They lying long shall not die windily;
Twisting on racks when sinews give way,
Strapped to a wheel, yet they shall not break;
Faith in their hands shall snap in two,
And the unicorn evils run them through;
Split all ends up they shan't crack;
And death shall have no dominion.

And death shall have no dominion.
No more may gulls cry at their ears
Or waves break loud on the seashores;
Where blew a flower may a flower no more
Lift its head to the blows of the rain;
Though they be mad and dead as nails,
Heads of the characters hammer through daisies;
Break in the sun till the sun breaks down,
And death shall have no dominion.

Clearly we do not here have the sort of point-for-point comparisons that we can make between the Cydnus passages in Plutarch and in *Antony*. But the subject is the same: death has no final power. We can go further: in both, death has no final power over man. To compare the poems, we simply start with the most obvious difference, or a striking feature of one we may not find so obvious in the other. Then we look for reasons. The clearest difference between these two poems is their length, the Donne poem being a fourteen-line sonnet, the Thomas poem three stanzas of nine lines each, almost twice the length. If we ask why, we are led straight into investigation of the subject matter in the two poems. Thomas's poem seems to be founded much more on feeling, and the emotional certainty perhaps takes time to realise itself. Donne's poem by contrast, seems much more of an argument, moving from point to point. It says that death is not mighty or dreadful and attempts to prove this via a list of arguments: 'Death is weak because (1) if sleep is pleasant, death must be more so; (2) the good (willingly) die young; (3) death is a slave to the occasions that produce it; (4) death keeps bad company; (5) drugs are better than death at giving us sleep; (6) after we die we rise again'. Each of these arguments could no doubt have been said at greater length, but Donne seems to want to make them as brief, and striking, as possible. If we compare Thomas's poem, we find that it does not say substantially different things from stanza to stanza. In the first stanza we learn that death is not final, that the dead will 'rise again' and become part of life: 'Dead men naked they shall be one / With the man in the wind and the west moon'. The second stanza tells us that however life and pain break us we are not finally broken. The third says that however things perish, one's essential identity remains. There seems no clear sequence of development as we see it in the Donne poem. This seems added to by the way each stanza begins and ends with the same line. Donne seems to set about proving a point, where Thomas simply assumes it. Thomas's poem starts from the same statement with which it ends.

This leads us to consider how exactly each poem denies death's power. Donne's argues that death will be a pleasure, then that it is feeble or contemptible and finally that we will rise again. Most of us, given that this is a 'Holy Sonnet' written by a seventeenth-century poet, are going to assume that Donne's basic exposure of death's weakness will stem from his Christian faith and his assurance of resurrection: we will tend to read the whole poem in the light of the argument it only really produces in its closing couplet. Actually most of the poem, if we consider closely, has been a series of arguments operating from quite secular or empirical premises. And what do we think of them? How forceful is the argument that if sleep, the image of death, is a pleasure, then death itself must be more so? How much do we really feel that death has been truly debased by the fact that it keeps company with poison, war and sickness? If these arguments are spurious, why offer them? Perhaps it is part of Donne's cheek: he addresses 'death' directly and with deliberately contemptuous familiarity, where Thomas is much more lofty in tone. Perhaps Donne *meant* his arguments to fail to convince, so that then we would realise that no merely human argument for death's weakness can work, and that the only convincing assault lies in a belief in Christian resurrection: thus the failure of the one would make us the more strongly feel the other. At any rate, however we look at it, the poem is dynamic, always moving towards a point.

If we consider we will see that there are many more 'things' in Thomas's poem; we have the man in the wind, the west moon, picked and clean bones, stars, elbow and foot and the sea, in stanza one alone. Donne, on the other hand, where he mentions data, mentions them as classes, or alternatives, or plurals – fate, chance, kings, desperate men, poison, war, sickness, 'poppy or charms'. Why? We can say that in Donne's poem they are parts of an argument, and therefore tend to be typical rather than individual. But we can extend the point further. Donne is engaged in a mental attack on death: he is putting his mind against it. Thomas seems much more concerned with the nature of life itself as an answer to death. He does not have to manipulate things into an argument: they are in a sense their own argument. Whatever is done to annihilate us cannot finally win, by the nature of things. Thomas's poem does at times seem to emerge from something like Christian belief, 'they shall rise again'; and the hymnic tone of the poem adds to this. But that belief seems more incidental, more a part of 'the rest of it', than in Donne, where its apparent incidentality at the end of the poem may have been a device.

So what is the principle that defeats death in Thomas's poem? If we look closely we can see that every point that is a 'taking away' is also one of being given something. The dead men naked will be one with the man in the wind and the west moon; when their bones are gone they shall have stars at elbow and foot, more or less giving them a stellar skeleton; though they are mad or dead their identity still hammers

through daisies. Sometimes this seems to go to the point of
contradiction:

> Twisting on racks when sinews give way,
> Strapped to a wheel, yet they shall not break;
> Faith in their hands shall snap in two,
> And the unicorn evils run them through;
> Split all ends up they shan't crack . . . .

If their bodies are broken, if their faith is snapped, if they are
overpowered by evil, what is there left not to break or crack?
Perhaps for Thomas the point is that the true self lies beyond
all that the self has – body, principles, love, sanity. The whole
poem, in contrast to Donne's, is full of images of dissolution,
of loss of reason, of form, of faith. Take away all that the self
has, it seems to imply, and we become part of the larger universe from which the self and its feelings and principles spring.

There is a striking point of comparison with Donne's poem
that may suggest itself here: Donne wants to have the self we
know survive ('One short sleep past, we wake eternally'),
where Thomas depicts the reduction of the old self. Donne
spends his whole poem belittling the physical fact of death;
Thomas allows death its full physical power in order to
demonstrate its ultimate weakness. But we had better be
careful of that word 'demonstrate' with Thomas, for in a sense
he demonstrates nothing. To state a principle would for him
be to defeat the object: death is only defeated through lived
experience; the whole victory of the poem depends on the loss
of the self's apartness; and that depends on the removal of
the kind of mental organising of experience that we see in
Donne's poem. Does that then explain why the poem is
without the form that Donne's shows? The rhyme scheme is
irregular or non-existent, the line lengths vary without pattern,
there seems no clear development from stanza to stanza; and
all the items in the poem, all the instances of continuance
through death, are not connected to one another save by the
most tenuous of links, as the pun on 'windily' suggests the
twisting of bodies on racks, or the 'dead as nails' moves on to
heads of characters hammering through daisies. We can take
this path, if we will.

By now we have got a fair amount out of the comparison,
and can continue if needed with analysis of the poems on their

own. We might, for example, wish to explore why Thomas uses images drawn from fantasy – the man in the wind (inversion of the man in the moon), the stars, the unicorn evils, the daisy hammers, the broken sun; or consider whether his serious and poetic tone is more effective than the more colloquial, if intellectually tenuous, approach of Donne. But the comparison has served even more purpose than to provide a way into the poems: it also gives us a unit of two quite different approaches to the same subject, and in that way extends our understanding of the range of possible poetic answers to death.

This level of comparison is as we said more challenging in that we may have to know of or find a second poem or work on the same theme, and also in that the points for comparison have to be thought out more by us. As can be seen, there is no single method for following out comparisons, for each text will suggest a particular procedure: but there is a *simple* method, and that is to start from the first thing that suggests itself and think it right through to the beginnings of analysis of the work, at or before which point other differences will suggest themselves and become incorporated in one's developing understanding. This applies also to much larger texts, where we do not have two passages or poems before us, but must select differences 'out of the air' as it were. This would be the case, for example, when comparing novels or novelists. If we were comparing the novels of, say, Hardy with Virginia Woolf, one might start from the fact that there seems to be much more plot in Hardy's novels, and follow this point out into the importance of the external world and of coincidence in Hardy as against the emphasis on the inner landscape of the psyche in Woolf; and thus to an entirely different notion of 'truth to life' in both novelists. If we were comparing Jane Austen to D. H. Lawrence, then the evident starting point would be the different attitudes to the portrayal of developing love relations. Once the grounds of comparison are selected, it is a matter of pursuing the different treatments in each author as far as they will take us.

As one last illustration here let us consider a situation where we have to work to isolate particular material for comparison. Suppose we were asked to compare Wordsworth to Pope – a fairly standard example, since the one is often taken as the prime examplar of English 'Augustan' or eighteenth-century poetry, and the other of that English 'Romantic' poetry which came into being partly through reaction against the Augustan mode. What contrasts can we find? Given that Pope wrote such a range of poetry, from the mock-heroic *The Rape of the Lock* to the emotional love poem *Eloisa to Abelard*, and from the satirical *Epistle to Dr Arbuthnot* to the philosophical *Essay on Man*; and that the same Wordsworth wrote the semi-comic 'Goody Blake and Harry Gill' as wrote the impassioned poetic autobiography *The Prelude*: where shall we start? Best to begin by taking each poet generally, or 'by feel', and we will get some distance. Pope, we may say, seems rather brisk and cool in tone, where Wordsworth is more emotional and sympathetic. Pope often seems to be mocking man in his poetry, whether laughing at the frailties of women in *The Rape of the Lock*, or at the ruling passion that makes fools of men in *An Essay on Man* or the *Moral Essays*, or at the empty pride that makes dull fools fancy themselves intellectuals or poets in *The Dunciad*. Wordsworth, however, rarely mocks, but seems to compassionate man in his suffering, from the old huntsman reduced to impotence in 'Simon Lee' to the wretched woman who laments on the hillside in 'The Thorn'. We could go further: Pope judges where Wordsworth sympathises. Further still: Pope often cuts human greatness or pride down to size or less; Wordsworth shows that the meanest of human lives is often the richest, whether in a beggar, an idiot, or the suffering of an abandoned countrywoman. Where Pope tends to shrink people, Wordsworth 'expands' them. Here we could even bring in Pope's *Eloisa to Abelard*, for there the two lovers are confined in separate religious houses where their passion baffles itself against their stony seclusion; or even the *Elegy to the Memory of an Unfortunate Lady*, where the grave reduces all that the lady once meant to dust; or the *Epistle to Miss Blount, on her leaving the Town, after the Coronation*, where a young girl whose head has been turned in the metropolis, is packed off for her own 'good' to the isolation of the country. Thus, working from 'this feel' can turn up valid contrasts which begin to draw the poetry into a larger whole.

We can pull in more. Pope's poetry, we may reflect, is all written in heroic couplets, with the sense often confined to the couplet. Wordsworth, however, frequently writes in blank verse and his sentences often go on for ten lines or more, spreading across line ends: this evidently fits with and extends the distinction we have been making between the two, whereby the one restricts or reduces, and the other elevates or expands. And there are other differences we can think of. Wordsworth's poetry is best known for being set in the country, and particularly in the Lake District: there is scarcely a poem that does not have some country setting, from the shepherd's cottage of *Michael* to the bleak tarn of *Resolution and Independence* or the woodland by night of 'The Idiot Boy': we find that when Wordsworth does set his poetry in the city, it is with reluctance, as during the time in London described in *The Prelude*, or when the city is asleep, as in 'Upon Westminster Bridge'. If we think, we will see that by contrast most of Pope's poems are set in the city or describe metropolitan attitudes, from the world of Hampton Court card-games in *The Rape of the Lock* to that of political or commercial life described in the *Moral Essays*.

Suppose, then, we do not stop there, but consider the preference in the one and the other for country or town settings – does it lead to any further differences? Well, in a town the concern is with man in society; in the country it can be, and with Wordsworth's poetry we see it *is*, the relation of man and his setting. There is scarcely a poem of Wordsworth's which does not portray the links between man and the landscape. Pope's poetry, we find, has a considerable social emphasis: and not just in portraying what is, but what should be. Pope, we find seems to think that man is best when he works with others, not when he is alone. If we consider all Pope's isolated figures, they are seen to be dangers – from the wilful Belinda, to the ambitious Sir Balaam in the *Moral Essays* or the vain poet Atticus in *An Epistle to Dr Arbuthnot*: all are accused by Pope of pride. And then we can think further: what else is under attack in *An Essay on Man* than the human pride by which man fancies to himself the right to question or search into the universe? What else is brought to our attention but the fact that the universe is so constituted that man has to cooperate as part of a larger social whole created by God? Yet in Wordsworth, by contrast, it is precisely the individual and the singular that are brought to our notice, from the singularity of Wordsworth's own personal experience as so fully described in *The Prelude*, to the individuality of attitude of the child in 'We are Seven', or the peculiarity of the story in 'Nutting': and more widely, Wordsworth's poetry deals most frequently with people on their own, removed from society. And thus we can go on. Pope's poetry, we find, is constantly harking back to past writers, particularly those of classical Greece and Rome, and citing them as examples or models. Wordsworth, however, makes no reference in his poetry to any tradition from which it springs: indeed his whole subject matter is in a sense revolutionary in that no one before had written with quite his degree of sympathy for rustic people in a wild setting. We can link this point about indebtedness to the point concerning society: it is of a piece with Pope's 'social' emphasis that he should place such stress on writing which is not singular but part of a 'society' of literary tradition.

All this we can say, and much more that is left out here, simply by starting from an initial general feeling and putting it into words and then pursuing its ramifications. But when it comes to the character of the two as poets, we really have to come to the point of setting two sample passages beside one another. It is not often easy to select 'representative' passages. There are those who might argue that we might as well put any two passages chosen at random together; but probably the most productive approach is to take two on broadly similar topics, if we can find them. Given the kinds of difference of subject matter we have already observed in Pope and Wordsworth, that may not seem very easy. Both, however, have written poems on the nature of man (though Wordsworth would not have put it this way): Pope's *Essay on Man* is just that, an attempt to understand man's place in the universe; and Wordsworth's *Prelude*, subtitled 'The Growth of a Poet's Mind', is effectively on a similar subject, since it considers the shaping influence of nature on the human spirit. Taking these two, what we need to find are two passages on similar enough topics for the *poetic* difference of the two to come through clearly.

Suppose we look for two passages where the philosophic centres of the poems are in some way set forth. An example from Pope is the one near the end of the first Epistle of *An Essay on Man*, describing God's relation to nature:

All are but parts of one stupendous whole,
Whose body, Nature is, and God the soul;
That, chang'd thro' all, and yet in all the same,
Great in th' earth, as in th' æthereal frame,
Warms in the sun, refreshes in the breeze,
Glows in the stars, and blossoms in the trees,
Lives thro' all life, extends thro' all extent,
Spreads undivided, operates unspent,
Breathes in our soul, informs our mortal part,
As full, as perfect, in a hair as heart;
As full, as perfect, in vile Man that mourns,
As the rapt Seraph that adores and burns;
To him no high, no low, no great, no small;
He fills, he bounds, connects, and equals all.

(I. 267–80)

As instance from Wordsworth we could take the description of the moment in *The Prelude* when, in crossing the Alps with a companion, Wordsworth is told by a peasant that far from having the highest point still ahead of them, they have just put it behind them: at this recorded shock '*that we had cross'd the Alps*', Wordsworth continues:

Imagination! lifting up itself
Before the eye and progress of my Song
Like an unfather'd vapour; here that Power,
In all the might of its endowments, came
Athwart me; I was lost as in a cloud,
Halted, without a struggle to break through.
And now recovering, to my Soul I say
I recognize thy glory; in such strength
Of usurpation, in such visitings
Of awful promise, when the light of sense
Goes out in flashes that have shewn to us
The invisible world, doth Greatness make abode,
There harbours whether we be young or old.
Our destiny, our nature, and our home
Is with infinitude, and only there;
With hope it is, hope that can never die,

Effort, and expectation, and desire,
And something evermore about to be.

                                                    (VI. 525–42)

Both passages suggest a God or divine force that operates
through nature on man. Pope, it is true, lays more stress on
the God who orders and energises this world, while
Wordsworth puts emphasis on the invisible world, from which
at such moments as the one he has experienced hints come of
the true home of his being: but each supposes a universe
instinct with deity.

Once we have got here, and established two key passages
of broadly similar subject, we can look for differences of
presentation. We see much more concrete detail in Pope: he
talks of earth, sun, breeze, stars, a hair, a heart. Wordsworth
mentions only a cloud, and that in an analogy. However,
Wordsworth is quite able to produce concrete detail in his
poetry, as the passage describing his descent of the Alpine
pass that follows this shows: what causes the absence of
sensuous detail in this passage is the fact that Wordsworth is
describing an experience where the visible world is no longer
present and his concentration is on a world beyond the senses.
That will make it significant that 'Imagination' starts the
passage: it is described as a 'vapour' as though it was a mist
that drove across his path on the mountain, but the very fact
that we suppose it a real mist and then realise that it is a
mental one the more surely drives us to awareness that the
invisible world is the subject. At any rate, the difference here,
of Pope having details from the solid world and Wordsworth
not, is attributable solely to a difference of orientation at this
particular point rather than to any significant distinction
between the two poets. So we must drop that line of approach
and continue.

The next difference we can notice is that Wordsworth relays
his experience as something he felt; and he declares, 'to my
Soul I say / I recognize thy glory'. Pope does not introduce
himself at all: he talks at most of 'us', but most often he is
simply describing God's relation to life. His statements bear
no question: they are absolutes, 'All are but parts of one
stupendous whole': he is handing down truths engraved on
tablets to us. Is it not then appropriate that he should be
writing in heroic couplets, where each unit of sense marches

with the rhyme, clear-cut, defined, immutable? And what is Wordsworth doing by contrast? Is not his passage relaying an immediate experience rather than a received truth? What Wordsworth is doing is finding out for himself something he had not known before; what Pope is doing is telling us what we have been too blind or arrogant to accept before. This is going to explain the much more tentative feel to Wordsworth's passage: the insight is in a sense occurring at the moment of writing. Wordsworth has no sooner written about their being told that they had crossed the Alps than 'Imagination!' lifts itself 'before the eye and progress of my Song': it is happening *now*. Yet, in a way, because he describes the imagination as like 'an unfathered vapour' that loses him as in a mist, we think that the experience occurred years ago on the mountain too. It is as though time collapses: the experience then is so vivid to him in writing about it that he relives it now: the act of writing is itself a part of his developing spiritual insight. And that is characteristic of Wordsworth: nothing can be fully real if it cannot in some sense be lived now. Nothing is real that is past. Life is always becoming, never quite reaching its true form, 'something evermore about to be'.

Maybe then that explains why it is that Wordsworth does not leave us with definite statements here. He often says two things where he might say one. What is 'the eye and progress of my Song'? It seems at once to be something that stays still and something that moves. Then we are told of 'such strength / Of usurpation . . . such visitings / Of awful promise', or 'Our destiny, our nature, and our home', or 'Effort and expectation and desire'. Either we say Wordsworth wrote vaguely, or that he deliberately refused us the kind of clarity that would in his view leave us with a fixed and dead truth. As we read, we have to relive the movements of his mind, a mind that is itself reliving its original experience. It has to be said, however, that observations such as these will not come to us easily at first.

Both the passages, from Pope and Wordsworth alike, seem full of energetic life. Pope's syntax beautifully gives an impression of the immediate activity of the creator. The whole passage, we may notice, is all one sentence: and certainly we feel the continuity and drive of the verse from beginning to end. And we can, albeit after long practice and thought, make something of this: if Pope is portraying the way that God is active throughout his creation, how better to do this than in one continuous sentence, which will imitate the divine pervasiveness, by which God, like the sentence itself, 'fills . . . bounds, connects, and equals all'? This can be taken further. The first and last couplets issue from the Creator himself, whereas the rest of the passage deals with his immediate activity within his creation, glowing in stars or breathing in our souls. In a sense the passage has a kind of circularity (perhaps a symbol of the perfection of God?), which 'bounds' the material it contains. And what of the changes we feel within the passage? God is described first through verbs: he warms, refreshes, glows, blossoms, and then, more generally, lives, extends, spreads, operates, breathes, informs. But then he is seen adjectivally, 'As full, as perfect, in a hair as heart; / As full, as perfect, in vile Man that mourns, / As the rapt Seraph that adores and burns'. The steady movement forward of the verse seems to be halted, drawn up in ranks as it were; a feeling increased by the way these lines start with identical phraseology. What can we say of this? it gives an impression of God both doing things and then being a state. And if we look back in the passage we may find a clue to this. Pope describes God as 'chang'd thro' all, and yet in all the same': in other words, he portrays God as at once altering and staying unchanged, or, to put it in more formal terms, as an 'unmoved mover'. And that is exactly what the syntax, first verbal, and then adjectival, enacts. More than this, we may see how Pope brings both together in the last couplet, 'To him no high, no low, no great, no small; / He fills, he bounds, connects, and equals all', where the first line is adjectival and the second composed of verbs.

Nevertheless, while Pope's syntax could be said so finely to imitate its subject, the action of God, that subject is still formally imitated within the heroic couplet, and is at an admiring remove from the poet. Not so Wordsworth's subject, which serves to break up even the comparative informality of his blank verse. No order here: only the reeling of an amazed psyche. The tenses of the verbs lurch from present to past and back again. The 'Imagination!' blurts itself upon the line in no less a manner than it suddenly strikes Wordsworth's spirit. The syntax staggers. The imagination actually seems to raise itself like a mist in the way that it is described through two and a half lines before being left suspended. The 'Here that' seems confusing; then the violence of the run-on line followed by the abrupt break, 'came / Athwart me', gives a heightened sense of dislocation; and this dislocation seems increased in the 'I was lost as in a cloud, / Halted, without a struggle to break through', where, apart from the lurch of 'Halted', the next phrase seems literally to have lost Wordsworth, for the 'I' has gone from it. Thereafter, the syntax seems slowly to become more certain, more rhythmic, as this new experience is gradually assimilated and understood. 'And now recovering': at first short, the syntax grows in length and assurance as it moves through tentative to more certain identification of the source and nature of what has happened to the poet.

The main difference evident from this, as said before, is that Pope keeps experience at arm's length (even when he describes himself, as in *An Epistle to Dr Arbuthnot*, it is through the medium of irony), where Wordsworth makes the interaction of self and world his subject: Pope wants to portray something, Wordsworth to live it. For Pope, God operates in an orderly mode within an ordered creation, best expressed in clear but carefully patterned verse. For Wordsworth, the nature of God or the 'imagination' is 'disorderly' and mysterious, forever revealing a reality whose connections with the self are deeper and stranger than one could ever have supposed: and for him this is naturally best 'imitated' ('recreated' might be a better word), in informal verse and varyingly indefinite diction, which can shape themselves in a moment to each changing and unpredictable experience.

Now, as said, we are unlikely at first to go anywhere near this distance in comparison. The description above, as in most of this book, is to show what can be done. Nevertheless, it should suffice to show how, when we have got one point of vantage on a work or works, when we have come to one tentative conclusion, we will find if we are 'right' that all other aspects of the text will begin to answer this conclusion, which they will illustrate and further in their own ways. In other words, if we are alert, any one insight will open up a host of others. Once start the car, and the rest of our task may, in time, be confined to steering.

7
Disjunctions

Disjunction is a part of all literature. We are always shocked
or jolted at the first moment as we shift from our own world
into encounter with another, however realistic. 'The Bottoms
had succeeded to Hell Row', 'It was the day of Bilbo's
eleventy-first birthday party', 'A widwe there was, somdel
stape in age / Was whilom living in a narwe cottage', 'Thou
still unravished bride of quietness', 'I am extremely concerned,
my dearest friend, for the disturbances that have happened
in your family', 'Gormenghast'. We then have to adjust to the
new world, to become immersed in it. Even then we may not
always be able to rest easy. Conditions we take for granted
can be violated; characters or landscapes of quite another
order from those to which we have acclimatised ourselves may
be put before us; assumptions we have made concerning the
laws governing the story may be suddenly taken away from
beneath us, as for instance in Swift's *A Modest Proposal for
Preventing the Children of Ireland from Being a Burden to their Parents
or Country*, where what we have assumed to be an honest man
outraged at the current poverty and wretchedness in Ireland
and trying to set out a humane remedy, turns out be be a
man proposing as that remedy the selling off by the poor of
many of their children as food.

Numbers of works of literature are founded on disjunctions,
or have a disjunctive method: the sudden shock of revelation
in masque or pantomime, the mixing of genres in tragi-comedy
or mock-heroic, the happy ending that emerges from the chaos
of comedy, the shock at the death of the hero in tragedy, or
the gap between one term and another in the conceits of
metaphysical poetry, as in comparing separated but spiritually
conjoined lovers to a pair of compasses, or weeping eyes to
baths, or loves to parallel lines. Works can be disjunctive by

being composed of many separate parts, whether the different books and subjects that make up Spenser's *Faerie Queene*, the manifold lyrics that form the body of Tennyson's *In Memoriam*, the four different voyages and contexts of Swift's *Gulliver's Travels*, the series of separate poetic sections in Eliot's *The Waste Land*, or even the several individual histories that constitute Isaac Asimov's science-fictional 'Foundation' series, or Keith Roberts's *Kiteworld*. A work with least disjunction is perhaps Samuel Richardson's *Clarissa*, where we are in immediate and continuous contact with the psyche of a heroine who stays the same throughout in her purity of resistance to the lecherous Lovelace: for thousands of pages we are kept in touch with the heroine's minute-by-minute experiences, with scarce any gap save for her sleep. Other works are more selective, and to this extent are more like a series of episodes, with causal strings slung between one and another. Such disjunctions in literature can often afford us a way of entering texts. They invite us, as we experience the shock they produce, to ask the question Why? and to go on to try to make sense of them, and thus perhaps of the whole work. The basic procedure employed, as in most of the cases described in this book, becomes one of 'making connections', of drawing what seem to be separated apprehensions into a new whole.

As first example we can consider Thomas Hardy's poem, 'The Voice':

> Woman much missed, how you call to me, call to me,
> Saying that now you are not as you were
> When you had changed from the one who was all to me,
> But as at first, when our day was fair.
>
> Can it be you that I hear? Let me view you, then,
> Standing as when I drew near to the town
> Where you would wait for me: yes, as I knew you then,
> Even to the original air-blue gown!
>
> Or is it only the breeze, in its listlessness
> Travelling across the wet mead to me here,
> You being ever dissolved to wan wistlessness,
> Heard no more again far or near?

Thus I; faltering forward,
Leaves around me falling,
Wind oozing thin through the thorn from norward,
And the woman calling.

If we ask ourselves what the subject of the poem is, we can say that Hardy is describing a dead woman whom he loved, and who in some sense seems to him to call from beyond the grave; but as the poem develops, he is not so sure of this, and asks whether he does not confuse her voice with the wind. The first two stanzas seem to describe a relationship, which is appropriate, since at this stage the woman is supposed actually to be calling.

But, if we think about it, the disjunction here is most strikingly seen and felt in the metre throughout the poem. In the first two stanzas it seems relatively regular and 'singable'. If we were to mark / for stressed syllables and × for unstressed, we have a pattern like this: 'Wŏmăn mŭch míssed, hŏw yŏu cáll tŏ mĕ, cáll tŏ mĕ, / Sáyĭng thăt nów yŏu ăre nŏt aš yŏu wére' and so on through the first seven lines in a regular metre of /××, which is known as dactylic measure. It has a lilting character that we could if we liked say fitted with the growing excitement of the speaker, as he feels the woman close and recalls their time together.

But then, if we notice, things begin to change. The last line of the second stanza is something like 'Evĕn tŏ thĕ ŏrigĭnăl air-blue gówn': there is still a dactylic element there, but it is largely lost. Then the first three lines of the third stanza have a largely dactylic metre but this goes in the broken metre of the last line, 'Heárd nŏ móre ăgain făr ŏr near'. The last line has only a ghost of the dactylic left: 'Thús I; fáltĕrĭng fórwărd, / Leáves ăround mĕ fálliňg, / Wind oózĭng thín through the thórn frŏm nórwărd, / Aňd thĕ wómăn cálliňg'. (Others may accentuate this slightly differently.) So we feel that the metre gets less rhythmic, more uneven throughout. What do we make of this? Given that we have seen how the subject of the poem is one of decreasing certainty on the part of the speaker that he is being called by the woman, given that his own view of the facts becomes bleaker through the four stanzas, we can relate the metrical alteration to the emotional one: just as he loses the belief that he is being addressed, and ends alone, so the lines lose their metrical certainty. The disjunction in the metre then becomes a way of heightening the disjunction in the subject. Paradoxically we are able to see how the form of the poem finely fits the content, even when that content describes a break.

If we look we will see that the disjunction is registered in other ways too. For most of the poem we have been looking at things via the speaker: we look through his eyes as he begs the woman to show herself, or asks whether 'she' is only the wind. But then in the last stanza we feel a shock as he suddenly turns round to look *at* himself: 'Thus I; faltering forward'. He seems to have become a tiny self now, seen from a distance, lost in bleak objectivity, fumbling his way over the cold marsh of life, viewed from above as a poor creature of limited insight. What does this shift do? We can say it is rather like the one where he gave up his illusion about the woman: now he refuses himself and us the assurance of his own mind, and appears a mere bewildered part of the inhospitable terrain of life. And as he does so, he becomes surrounded by a landscape, almost lost in it – the wet mead, the falling leaves, the oozing wind. And yet still, at the end of all this, we find Hardy turning back to reverse our presuppositions yet again. The woman whose voice was doubted now still exists: 'And the woman calling'. But in a sense her existence is harsher than her not being there at all: she calls, but he can no longer distinguish her voice, and she does not seem to be calling to him, just aimlessly calling, as though both she and he now pursued their separated activities.

A more complex example of disjunction is to be seen in Swift's celebrated *Modest Proposal*, briefly mentioned earlier. Here as we said we make assumptions about the proposer which become undermined. We think at first he is a man with a genuine social conscience:

> It is a melancholy object to those who walk through this great town or travel in the country, when they see the streets, the roads and cabin doors crowded with beggars of the female sex, followed by three, four, or six children, all in rags, and importuning every passenger for an alms. These mothers, instead of being able to work for their honest livelihood, are forced to employ all their time in strolling to beg sustenance for their helpless infants; who, as they grow up, either turn thieves for want of work; or leave their dear native country, to fight for the Pretender in Spain, or sell themselves to the Barbadoes.

He goes on to say that whoever, in these distresses, could find a way of making these children 'sound and useful members of the commonwealth' would deserve to have 'his statue set up for a preserver of the nation'. So far we probably think of him as a compassionate man with a burning urge to help his fellows. And this goes on even as he begins to compute the number of breeding couples in Ireland and the number of children born annually. The statistics seem cold, but then in order to approach the situation realistically, we suppose, they are necessary. But actually these statistics have been leading in quite another direction:

> I have been assured by a very knowing American of my acquaintance in London; that a young healthy child, well nursed, is, at a year old, a most delicious, nourishing and wholesome food, whether stewed, roasted, baked or boiled; and, I make no doubt, that it will equally serve in a fricasie, or ragoust.

He then proceeds to his scheme for organised butchery of infants for their meat, like cattle. By this means, he claims, the Irish will at last have a home-grown manufacture which they can sell on the open market for their and their nation's profit.

Our immediate reaction to this of course is one of shock. But we ought to be honest about this shock. It is not just a case of having been tricked by the story or the proposer. We have also let ourselves be taken in. And we had better consider how and in what way. So, looking back, we see how we ignored the sinister side of the proposer. The 'melancholy object' he described was not sympathy for the poor, but exasperation at their uselessness: and, incidentally at their importunity. The way he talked about them in numbers and reduced them to computations was not as a means of helping them but actually as a form of dehumanisation before they were treated as cattle. And perhaps we are led to reflect that such reduction of people to numbers helps all inhuman schemes, not least the Nazi holocaust. By making these links we may begin to see that it is not just some nasty proposer who is under attack here, but that the indictment spreads to ourselves. We, by our own complacent assumptions, are in some way analogous to all who have ignored the Irish situation. Reality is jagged, and discontinuous, Swift then is saying: the real enemy is any settled assumption.

To show this, we find that he proceeds to undermine our 'new' awareness too. Now that the proposer has exposed his scheme, we may feel him a monster. Swift however does not leave us there. Surely, we may feel, there are better schemes than this? But we find that the proposer is ready for us: 'let no man talk to me of other expedients' he says, and goes on to list every other practical remedy under the sun: nothing of this will work, he says, because it invites a reform of behaviour which is out of the question. His scheme will work because it appeals immediately to self-interest. Ask any Irishman whether he would rather have been sold for food at a year old than live as he has had to, and he will answer in the affirmative. The proposer's remedy will at a stroke clear up the misery of underproduction and overpopulation; it will make husbands and wives much happier with one another; it will make the kingdom wealthy, and since the goods are of its own manufacture, relatively self-sufficient. And is it not the case, the proposer implies at one point, that butchering infants would not be so cruel as with older children, since infants have no foresight and little knowledge of what is happening to them? And the greatest question of all is also implicit. If the Irish have been reduced, both through their own behaviour and by that of the English, to the condition of animals, why not treat them as animals? What is man that we should regard him as immutable or incapable of descending to a beast? We may recall here that Swift portrays just such degraded men in the form of his Yahoos in Book Four of *Gulliver's Travels*, where the equine race, the Houyhnhnms, normally considered by man to be at the level of cattle, are the ideal, and treat the Yahoos as brutes, even considering in council whether or not to exterminate them.

Now most of us are going to read the entirety of the proposal with a sense of shock at the proposer, but little more. We are going to feel that Swift lulls us into a sense of false security in order to increase our sense of outrage at this proposer when his true objective becomes apparent. We are not at first going to see that the object of the shock is to disturb *our* complacency. And as for the rest of the proposal, it is going to be the same: the proposer's horrible scheme is there to show us the only remedy left if we do not use more compassionate means: and of course it is an absurd and hateful remedy. To take this view, however, is not to allow the disjunctions their full force, to insist on a simple reading which will leave the proposer the creature of outer darkness, and us able to rest in comfortable moral disdain of him. But suppose at the end we are left with the yawning questions that are there: (1) what other realistic alternative is there? (2) who would the Irish thank – us for our compassion, or him for a scheme which, however it offends our sensibilities, works? (3) are we so sure, we who gladly eat veal or lamb, that the degraded Irish are so human, or even that humanity itself is quite other than bestial? (4) can we be certain that we do not find some sneaking assent to the proposer's scheme, given such things as the ignorance of babies, the convincing authority of statistics, and the evident benefits that it will achieve? And last, and having opened ourselves to all these questions, we come to the final disjunction, the last shift of ground that turns all these things back on us: who are we that we have entertained such ideas? What sort of people are we that we can go along for whatever benefit with this reduction of people to useful commodities? If we read the satire while ignoring the potential direction of the several disjunctions it contains, we will remain comfortably assured that only the proposer is under attack and we are safe. If we allow the satire its full scope we will find that our habit of accepting what we are given is continually undermined until we are forced to confront ourselves: first we accept the projector, then we reject him, then we begin to wonder whether he may not be right after all, and then we look at ourselves and find the gaze of Adolf Eichmann returning ours. Our ignorance will not save us; our openness to the text and subsequent self-scrutiny may lacerate us; but at least in the latter case we may learn something.

The disjunction we earlier traced in looking at Hardy's 'The Voice' adds only to a sense we already had, fits in with an impression of the poem already set up in us. It is much harder when we are faced with disjunctions that run counter to all that we have assumed, as with the example from Swift. There is also a striking example of this at the end of Chaucer's long romantic poem *Troilus and Criseyde*, where the poet, who may earlier have seemed to portray the love of the Trojan

Troilus for the Greek Criseyde with great sympathy, even to the point of forgiving Criseyde for yielding to the blandishments of the Greek Diomede and thereby betraying Troilus (Bk v, 1093–9), suddenly turns round and tells us that this is what comes of pagan lust and ignorance of Christ, and that all modern lovers should turn themselves away from mere fleshly appetite to devotion to Him who died for us on the Cross (Bk v, 1828–55). It is a pretty striking apparent volte-face, and one that we may not care to give weight, preferring to see it as a sudden lurch on the poet's part, or the product of a testy narrator who feels the tragedy of the loss of all that was good in the love, rather than look back to consider whether our previous sympathy for Troilus and Criseyde may not have been sentimental and inaccurate, and whether there is more of condemnation of them in the poem than we previously thought. At this level disjunctions can drive us to a deeper understanding of a work, rather than reinforcing one we already have. But we have to be ready to admit them and not dismiss them in any facile way.

A further example of this occurs in Wordsworth's *The Prelude* (1805). It – the disjunction itself, that is – is the episode describing the love relation between one Vaudracour and Julia at the end of Book IX. It takes up not far short of half of a very important book in the poem describing Wordsworth's experience of the French Revolution. He has told us of how he went to France at the time of the Revolution's early fervour, of how he became caught up in its enthusiasm, and made a friend of one Michel Beaupuy with whom he would engage in long political discussions. But then in the midst of describing these discussions, Wordsworth abruptly breaks off to tell us that 'I shall not, as my purpose was, take note / Of other matters which detain'd us oft / In thought or conversation . . .',

> . . . but I will here instead
> Draw from obscurity a tragic Tale
> Not in its spirit singular indeed
> But haply worth memorial, as I heard
> The events related by my patriot Friend
> And others who had borne a part therein.
>   (IX.543–5, 550–5)

There then ensues the long story of how the young Vaudracour, of noble birth, fell in love with the meaner Julia from the same French town. Vaudracour's family disapproved and their relationship had to be hidden. But eventually Julia became pregnant, and her family sent her to another town until the baby was born in secret. Thither Vaudracour followed her, and they determined that he should return to his father and try to secure some money, perhaps in the form of a filial portion, by means of which they could find some solitary place to live. Back at home, however, Vaudracour did not ask for money as planned. But he made his father sufficiently aware of his determined love for Julia, and in response his parent threatened him 'that by a mandate / Bearing the private signet of the State / He should be baffled in his mad intent, / And that should cure him' (ll. 665–8). After this, Vaudracour went about armed. Then his parents pretended some reason for having to go to their country seat and left him alone in the house. One night three armed men set upon him at the door: he, enraged, killed one and wounded another, for which he was imprisoned. (The narrative is not clear, but one is to assume that the three men were hired by Vaudracour's father and that the object was to drag him off to confinement.)

Meanwhile, left alone, Julia is near-suicidal with anxiety. Through the help of a friend, Vaudracour is released from prison, and is able to return to his father's house provided he harbours no more thoughts of Julia. But within a few days he can stand it no longer and returns to Julia. There he tells her that they cannot be united, as he is a murderer. Meanwhile once again his father is bent on preventing his son's love, and Vaudracour is eventually arrested. However, intercession by the local magistrate minister ensures his release and return to Julia in her confinement. Vaudracour is now a despondent man, unable to propose any lasting relationship to Julia, and eventually her parents conclude that since Vaudracour's father remains obdurate about marriage, the only course for Julia is to enter a convent; and this, eventually, after she has for the last time asked Vaudracour to elope with her, is what she does. Vaudracour himself takes on the care of their child, returning with it to a cottage in the country. But, 'after a short time, by some mistake / Or indiscretion of the Father', the child dies. Thereafter Vaudracour remains a gloomy recluse till his death.

Now all this convoluted story seems to have nothing whatever to do with the French Revolution or indeed with any personal concern of Wordsworth's. Everything else he describes in *The Prelude*, his choice of subject-matter for a poem, his childhood, the growth of his imagination, his experience of Cambridge, the Alps, London, France, England at war, is portrayed as it affected him. Only here does he introduce a narrative of third parties. So the story is certainly anomalous on this count, quite apart from the abruptness with which it is forced on our notice. And perhaps we will not find it a very well-told story either. Vaudracour's father becomes something of a monster as he sets hired bravoes on his own son and uses the law against him. And do we feel very happy with Vaudracour's behaviour? It might be said that he is rather lacking in resolve: why did he not ask his father for money? If he really loved Julia, could he not have found some way of eloping with her? Why was the money such an object? Or we might want to ask why he felt so guilty about killing one of the three men: we do not perhaps see enough into his mind to realise why he should be so troubled at this. If he is to be seen as increasingly a melancholic, then perhaps a clearer portrayal of the fact might have helped. And at the end, we may well find the account of the child's death puzzlingly terse: it seems described in a 'throwaway' manner, and yet we have been told that the child meant everything to Vaudracour. So both as an anomaly within the context of the entire *Prelude*, and on its own terms, the story of Vaudracour and Julia can jolt us. Why then did Wordsworth put it in?

There have been those – this is offered as mere information – who have said that the whole story is a disguised account of Wordsworth's own relationship in France with one Annette Vallon, by whom he had a child at this time, before leaving her and returning to England. Wordsworth, it is said, at first felt he had had to put this episode into the poem, for it was an important part of his autobiography. But, married as he was to an English lady at the time of writing (Mary Hutchinson), he had to disguise the account. Later editions of *The Prelude* dropped the story, which appeared as a separate poem: by then, it is suggested, Wordsworth had come to realise that his relationship with Annette, while important in his development, did not contribute greatly to the growth of his poetic mind. We can settle for this explanation if we wish. It does leave the poem something of an amalgam though; and it is itself largely conjecture.

Suppose, however, we consider it simply as part of the material of the poem itself. The jolt we feel when we come to it need not drive us to an extraliterary explanation for it. Rather, we could ask whether the very disjunction it makes us feel should not impel us to try to relate it more closely to the poem. And that will mean some interpretation of it in the poem's own terms. To what other aspect of the poem is it in any way similar? Thinking this way, we could, for instance, see it as a kind of symbol in amorous terms for what is going on and is to go on in the Revolution. What might alert us to this, for example, is the fact that the story begins just where Wordsworth has been discussing with Beaupuy the iniquity of 'captivity by mandate without law' by the state, and in a short time we are to hear how Vaudracour's father threatens a 'mandate' without law against him.

Encouraged by this similarity, we may look for other parallels. Suppose, for instance, we were to say that the first raptures of Vaudracour's love for Julia,

> Earth liv'd in one great presence of the spring,
> Life turn'd the meanest of her implements
> Before his eyes to price above all gold . . .

are not altogether unlike the joys Wordsworth finds among the European nations in the early stages of the Revolution itself:

> Oh! most beloved Friend, a glorious time
> A happy time that was; triumphant looks
> Were then the common language of all eyes:
> As if awak'd from sleep, the Nations hail'd
> Their great expectancy . . . .
>
> (VI, 681–5)

As said, the urge to make such connections comes precisely from the gap between the two accounts, of Wordsworth's experience of the Revolution and then this oddly impersonal romantic tale. We are driven to try to make some links between the anomalous story and the rest of the poem, since otherwise it will be a mere irrelevant-seeming appendage, and the only one of its kind in the poem. Had the poem as a whole been a poorer or more frequently digressive work, the urge would not have arisen. It may be a mistaken urge: any poem has after all a right to its own defects. But if it yields results, it is worth having followed it through.

So far we have got to the point of seeing that Vaudracour's amorous fervour might be paralleled by the revolutionary fervour described elsewhere in the poem. Now we can perhaps begin to think of the whole process of his story and that of the Revolution. Wordsworth's account of the Revolution in Books Nine and Ten of *The Prelude* is of something that goes bad. First of all there is popular enthusiasm and a great burst of feeling and the breaking of old bonds. But then come threats to the Revolution from invading foreign armies; and later the Revolution begins further to establish itself through the execution of enemies. The Terror grows, and with it tyranny and repression: slowly the Revolution loses its early fervour, its ideals become whittled away into expediences, and at length it begins to assume the aspect of the very despotism it overthrew. If we put the story of Vaudracour and Julia beside this, there is some parallel. During the course of his amorous experience Vaudracour is reduced to a 'burnt-out case', a melancholy recluse unable to converse any more with his fellow-man: he has let Julia go, and the child, the hope for the future, has died. Vaudracour's father, the 'old tyranny', is not overcome: his remorseless refusal to some extent crushes the love of Vaudracour and Julia. In a way we could argue that Vaudracour and Julia are especially revolutionaries in that they practise one of the central ideals of the Revolution – class *égalité*, the noble Vaudracour coming together with the poorer Julia. Seen in this way, the story of Vaudracour and Julia becomes a metaphor for the whole process by which the French Revolution began, struggled and finally lost itself.

But then it may well be asked, why spend half a book producing a metaphor for something that is described clearly enough in literal terms anyway? The parallels may be there, but do they throw fresh light on what is going on? Perhaps they do in that the story suggests that maybe the class system can never finally be overthrown, even in the hearts of those who try to defy it. The tyrannous father then becomes simply an externalisation of an incapacity in Vaudracour. And that there is such incapacity is also suggested by Vaudracour's curious failures of individual decision and feeling, whether in not asking his father for money, or not eloping with Julia, or not at least showing sorrow even at his final parting from Julia. Nevertheless, even this is not sufficient to make the story seem fully organic to the poem, and one is driven to look for further links.

At least, that is one way of putting the sequence: it may equally be that we bring to the tale an already half-found hypothesis as to what else in the poem it might relate to. Since the tale itself is on any interpretation a fiction or disguise, it would seem best to go with something else that is disguised in this poem. Suppose we were to consider not the Revolution itself but Wordsworth's own reaction to it .... There is not the space here to go deeply into this, and the material involved would properly belong to another chapter. But we could consider that there is evidence that Wordsworth himself was not as impassioned about the Revolution as he might have us believe. That is, there is disjunction between his ostensible and his real commitment. When first he arrives in France, he sets about 'affecting more emotion than I felt' (IX.71). He wonders at his own lack of involvement with the fervour about him; puts it down first to the fact that he is ill-informed about events; and second, contradictorily, to his being so used to the ideals of the Revolution from his own democratic Lake District upbringing that he could not find them other than a matter of course here (IX.85–110, 217–53). We are going to find these admissions something of a shock. Later he becomes involved with Beaupuy and has ardent discussions with him concerning the approaching New Jerusalem; but not so ardent that Wordsworth does not find his mind slipping away from 'earnest dialogues' to contemplate the romantic nature of the woods around in which they are occurring, or even to regret the ruin of castle or convent, the very symbols of monarchic and ecclesiastical despotism against which the Revolution opposed itself (IX.438–503). It is Beaupuy who commits himself actively to the cause of the Revolution, and is eventually killed fighting for it; while Wordsworth, fastidiously careful of his poetic genius, returns to England amid a cloud of excuses (he says he had no money, that he could have done no good, that it would have been a waste (x.190–202)). We can find analogy for all this in the story of Vaudracour and Julia. Vaudracour seems very fervent in his love for Julia, but actually proves curiously inert and finally almost indifferent. So too Wordsworth with the Revolution. In this way we can tie the anomalous-seeming romantic tale back into the fabric of the poem while at the same time understanding something more about the poem itself. But it has to be said that there are many who would dissent from such a reading.

Enough now has perhaps been illustrated of disjunction generally. What we will now do is look closely at one particular form of it – inconsistency.

8
Inconsistencies

It is quite often the case that some form of inconsistency is present in a work, and this, when detected and explored, can provide a very productive way of opening the text and sometimes finding more in it than we could ever have supposed. Whenever some form of argument occurs in a work, inconsistency may well be found by simply looking at how well the argument holds together. The most common other form that inconsistency takes is when a work is not true to its own terms. We may not feel the inconsistency in an argument until we look at it closely. However we do feel the inconsistency where a happy or sad ending to a story is forced on it when it seemed to be going the other way, or when too many coincidences are used to alter a character's life, or simply when the 'ground rules' of a text are violated.

Consider the following, 'The Little Black Boy', from the *Songs of Innocence* of William Blake:

My mother bore me in the southern wild,
And I am black, but O! my soul is white;
White as an angel is the English child,
But I am black, as if bereav'd of light.

My mother taught me underneath a tree,
And sitting down before the heat of day,
She took me on her lap and kissed me,
And pointing to the east, began to say:

'Look on the rising sun: there God does live,
'And gives his light, and gives his heat away;
'And flowers and trees and beasts and men receive
'Comfort in morning, joy in the noonday.

'And we are put on earth a little space,
'That we may learn to bear the beams of love,
'And these black bodies, and this sunburnt face
'Is but a cloud, and like a shady grove.

'For when our souls have learn'd the heat to bear,
'The cloud will vanish; we shall hear his voice,
'Saying: "Come out from the grove, my love & care,
' "And round my golden tent like lambs rejoice." '

Thus did my mother say, and kissed me;
And thus I say to little English boy:
When I from black and he from white cloud free,
And round the tent of God like lambs we joy,

I'll shade him from the heat, till he can bear
To lean in joy upon our father's knee;
And then I'll stand and stroke his silver hair,
And be like him, and he will then love me.

Most evidently this seems a happy song of love and togetherness. The black boy expresses his sorrows and his mother
comforts him, gives him back a sense of belonging in the
world. The argumentative direction of the poem, its certainty
of tone, the emotional context of a mother consoling her child,
the fact that this is called a Song of Innocence, would all
suggest that we look no further. Yet what can be maintained
here is that the very existence of an argument in a work should
be an invitation to us to probe it. And what happens here if
we do? Probably not much at first, since the process is a hard
one. But gradually we may begin to feel that there is something
just a little strange perhaps in the fact that the mother talks
about God giving his light and heat away to all so that they
receive comfort and joy, and then tells her son that we are
put on earth so that we may learn to *bear* the beams of this
love. Why should they have to be borne if they give such joy?
And then we might ask, *do* they give such joy in the tropics
or the southern wild? The sun there is often a burning,
enervating or destructive force. It may occur to us too that
the mother is telling her son all this while sitting down in the

shade of a tree before the heat of day: plain sunlight would not give her much joy. Should we perhaps just ignore these thoughts, and see the weakness of the argument here as the kind of inconsistency inherent in the fact of living? Perhaps we will want to. But we may find it more revealing to go on to look at other aspects of the argument – not in any iconoclastic glee, but simply in search of the truth of what is going on.

The mother's argument is that coloured people have their dark skins to protect them from the full intensity of God's heat/love. In plain physical fact this is tenuous. And we might wonder how she can think of the soul in the same physical terms as the body, like a little white lump surrounded by a protective shell. She seems certainly rather a materialist in the way she thinks. And we might go on to say the same of her conflation of physical sunlight and heat with metaphysical love. Then we could enter a whole area of speculation. The mother says that the black body is a kind of filter, not just a shade. She says that it both protects the soul and lets through some heat to it. 'When our souls have learn'd the heat to bear', she says, the body will come off. It is rather reminiscent of Tom in Kingsley's *The Water-Babies* losing the 'husk' of his old blackened body when he enters the stream and swims away as a tiny water-baby. The soul will, as it were, have been 'done to a turn' – will be, if we want to take it to literal lengths, now as black as the body that originally contained it. It might occur to us that this does not quite fit with the black boy's insistence on his soul being 'white' in the first stanza: there whiteness seems something good, a sign of spiritual acceptability; how could a black soul square fully with that feeling? But more than this, if we consider, we will see that the mother is saying that when our souls are 'ready', we will die and go to heaven: that is what she means by the cloud vanishing and God calling to the boy to come out from his grove. To which we may ask: is that really what life is like? Do we only die when our souls are ready? Is it not the case that many people die young, or in unrepented evil? We begin to feel that the mother is imposing a pattern on life which its often random or chaotic character will not admit. And then it might strike us as rather odd to consider us as growing spiritually better the older we get. It would surely be false to pretend that old black men are all spiritually more advanced than young ones. Some of them can be much more evil. And, reading back, we are forced to object too that old black men are not in any case better able to bear heat and sun than young ones: indeed in reality the old probably find the sun more intolerable and debilitating. If we ask where those difficulties spring from, we begin to see that it has something to do with the mixing up of the physical and the spiritual by the mother. Black bodies are shades protecting souls being slowly made ready to bear God's heat/love: from this and the time factor, the implication has to follow that the older you are, the better, which in fact is false.

And so we can proceed. Consider, for instance, the picture of the black and white boy in heaven. The white boy is described as not yet having learnt to bear the heat of God's love, from which the black boy can lovingly protect him. Yet can we be happy with a predicament in which one child has learnt to bear God's love before death and the other not? Is this not a kind of reverse colour-prejudice, whereby God has given more of his love to black boys? And on the assumption that we only go to heaven when we have learnt to fear God's love, what is the white boy doing there? At this point, we might begin to ask almost mathematical questions about black versus white as a spiritual umbrella. If black lets through less heat, then is it not implied that white lets through more? But we may suppose that there is more heat about in the southern wild than in temperate England. Then if the difference in the strength of the sun's heat was matched by the difference in the permeability of the skins, the white boy might have learnt to bear the heat he has been given just as much as the black boy has his. In other words, there is no reason why white boys in heaven should necessarily be spiritually frailer than black boys. Why then, has the black boy chosen to portray the white one in this way? Along these lines our minds might move, with varying degrees of amusement at the peculiar speculations we have been driven to, probably with some sense that such enquiries really get us nowhere, or that they look too closely at a simple poem and leave it worse than it was. Perhaps we have something of the feeling about the intellect ironically portrayed by Swift in the 'Digression

Concerning Madness' in section IX of his *A Tale of a Tub*, 'In the proportion that credulity is a more peaceful possession of the mind than curiosity, so far preferable is that wisdom, which converses about the surface, to that pretended philosophy which enters into the depth of things, and then comes gravely back with informations and discoveries, that in the inside they are good for nothing'.

But really, if we consider, there may indeed be a reason we could find for some of the oddities we have noticed. What is the little black boy's mother trying to do? She is trying to console him for the sense of aching exclusion and alienation he describes in the first stanza. There he says that the English boy is white as an angel, but he is black, as though bereaved or cut off from life. It will not be hard for us to see the mother's story as a compensation, and indeed one which goes entirely in the opposite direction. Blackness, she says, is not a sign of exclusion at all, but a special mark of God's care and love. Black boys receive more of God's love than white boys: this conclusion is reached by identifying God's love with the sun's heat. And so on, until far from being a meaningless world of outer darkness, the black boy's life and his colour are divinely privileged, and the whole of his existence is carefully and providentially planned as a means of providing happiness on earth and bliss in heaven. Such a consolation we must find no less extreme than the black boy's earlier despair. But we see the main fact: his mother, as his mother, desperately wants to make her boy happy, make him feel he belongs. When we make ourselves aware of this context, it will be easy for us to relate the inconsistencies of her argument back to this central human impulse: she will bend anything to turn life into an extension of her own maternal instincts, a place where there will be only laughter, joy and security.

What then do we make of the black boy's response to her story? He has evidently accepted it uncritically: more, he has added to it the picture of himself looking after the white boy in heaven. If the mother's story is a questionable fiction, he turns it to delusion. If we look carefully, we will see that the mother is much more concerned with God's care for black people, but her son is interested rather in how her myth of divine favour will enable him to be friends with the white boy, 'And be like him, and he will then love me'. It is natural after

all: children want friends of their own age! But in the case of
the black boy we see how it comes from that initial sense of
exclusion from companionship with the white boy that he
recorded in the first stanza. In that stanza he described a
feeling that rose naturally from his life's experience. But the
consolation he feels at the end of the poem arises only from a
fictional view of life which we have seen to be internally
inconsistent and untenable. Doubtless, we might reflect, Blake
could have given the mother a consoling myth for her son
which would have been less immediately questionable. She
could, for instance, have said that life is hard but suffering
brings us nearer to the suffering of a loving God, and then
perhaps offered heaven as a consolation. Instead she – or
rather Blake through her – gives us a story so weak in itself
that no justifiable consolation can be drawn from it. Why is
this? We could say that Blake wants to give us a portrait in
self-delusion: the mother deludes herself and her son, and he
goes on to compound this in self-delusion. This would be to
look at the poem rather satirically. The poem is so constituted
that we are more likely to be driven back to ask ourselves
where the truth is to be found. If the consolations are false,
we are more inclined to find the pains that prompted them,
the pain of exclusion and blackness described in the first
stanza, as the experience that is more real, the one that will
not really go away.

Whether by this route, or whether simply by looking at the
poem and wondering at its sequence, we may be struck by
the fact that the first stanza is not in the past but in the
present tense. We would assume that since on the surface of
it the black boy is consoled by his mother's story, then the
first stanza and the feeling it records should be in the past
tense, since they have been wiped away. Thus one might have
looked for something along the lines of 'I felt black while at
the same time feeling my soul to be white; I felt that the
English child was as white as an angel while I was something
dark and excluded from life. But then my mother calmed
me. . .'. Instead it is, 'And I am black, but O! my soul is
white;/White as an angel is the English child,/But I am black,
as if bereav'd of light'. In other words, we must feel that the
present tense used gives an aspect of permanence to these
feelings; and this of course is heightened by the sense that any

happier feelings in the poem are on the evidence willed self-delusion. So, whatever he says at the end about the happy times coming in heaven, the present tense of the first stanza reminds us that the feelings of rejection that it records are at least as real if not more so. And we may go further: the fact that the poem thus inconsistently begins and ends with the present tense may suggest to us a circularity; may hint that after all the consolations the black boy will slip back once more into the despair with which the poem began; may imply that his early life at least is one long warfare between the painful feelings given by experience and the pleasing ones afforded by any fiction in which he can find temporary relief. If we look at the poem in this way, it becomes a tragic human portrait: certainly something quite different from what we normally suppose of a Song of Innocence. And all this has come from simply observing the inconsistencies of the argument on which the poem is based.

The same technique can be applied to the apparently successful argument concerning divine providence at the end of Chaucer's *The Knight's Tale*, as uttered by Duke Theseus of Athens in his attempt to assuage the general grief at the tragic death of the young hero Arcite: given sufficient leisure to attend closely to what Theseus is saying, we may ask whether he does in truth succeed in proving the existence of a God, or in proving life divinely ordered, when he refers simply to the fact that everything dies, or calls life a prison. Or in Shakespeare's *Coriolanus* we might closely inspect the argument used by the patrician Menenius to calm the incensed Roman mob who feel that the senate is holding back corn while they starve. Menenius describes the whole state as a body composed of many members, and figures the senate as the belly, which first receives all the food that the body needs and then sends it out; he claims that the rest of the body thereby receives 'the flour of all, / And leave[s] me but the bran'. We might ask whether it could ever be true that the belly lives on inferior food to the rest of the body. The fact that Menenius thus reverses the citizens' picture of the senate as rapacious to one of the senate as starved (certainly not true on the evidence of our own eyes) is itself highly suspect.

These, of course, are still situations in which a fictive view of events is being used to pacify, as in 'The Little Black Boy':

but there are other and barer arguments just as open to question on grounds of inconsistency – some of the poems of Donne or Cleveland, for example, or several eighteenth-century works. Pope's *Essay on Man*, for instance, we may find shot through with inconsistencies, and not of the sort that would lead us to find the poem more subtly organised. Thus, we might want to ask how it is that Pope, who has described man as created by God an inherently restless creature, can then go on to *blame* man for being restless. The whole poem is directed at telling man to accept his lot, not to seek to change himself or to find out more than is good for him simply to exist. We might also ask how if that is so, how if that had been universally followed by man, he could have developed into the state of civilisation in which Pope evidently so much rejoices. Or we might wonder, if Pope is so concerned in the poem to warn man against aspiring to the condition of angels, that he himself violates the sacred 'chain of being' in another direction by proving by how much man is inferior to the beasts. And so on, with many more questions. Ask one, and others will begin to occur. And even if such questions lead us to a less admiring view of a work, they will have revealed what is to us more of the truth about it.

But inconsistency takes many forms. It can, for instance, occur in apparent shifts of mood or feeling, rather than of attitude or argument. Arnold's *Dover Beach* is an example here. The poem begins,

> The sea is calm tonight.
> The tide is full, the moon lies fair
> Upon the straits; – on the French coast the light
> Gleams and is gone; the cliffs on England stand,
> Glimmering and vast, out in the tranquil bay.
> Come to the window, sweet is the night-air!

So far we seem to have a happy and peaceful scene: a sense of richness and abundance appears to pervade it, with the calm sea, the full tide, the fair moon, the light coming and going and the sweet night air to which the poet invites his beloved. Yet now we find the lines continue:

> Only, from the long line of spray
> Where the sea meets the moon-blanch'd land,

Listen! You hear the grating roar
Of pebbles which the waves draw back, and fling,
At their return, up the high strand,
Begin, and cease, and then again begin,
With tremulous cadence slow, and bring
The eternal note of sadness in.

It certainly seems at variance with the earlier happy lines. We might feel at first perhaps that the 'Only . . . .' suggests no more than a slight exception to the general rule: but then, as the syntax lengthens, pulled across line ends, it seems to drag deeper into a sense of melancholy, and we hear of a moon-blanch'd land and a grating roar leading to 'The eternal note of sadness'. How are we to understand this? Has the poet simply shifted his mood? Or when he speaks of 'The eternal note of sadness' does he mean that sadness is more real than joy, that sadness maybe lies through and beyond experience of joy?

Certainly we find that the mood of the poem now grows steadily darker. In the next stanza the poet moves on to describe how

Sophocles long ago
Heard it on the Aegean, and it brought
Into his mind the turbid ebb and flow
Of human misery.

We seem to have gone further into gloom here, from the faintly elegiac 'sadness' to the harsher 'misery'. And in the next stanza the mood has become bleaker still, as the poet shifts to contemplate not just recurrent human misery but the final loss in his age of the religious faith that might have assuaged that misery:

The Sea of Faith
Was once, too, at the full, and round earth's shore
Lay like the folds of a bright girdle furl'd.
But now I only hear
Its melancholy, long, withdrawing roar,

> Retreating, to the breath
> Of the night-wind, down the vast edges drear
> And naked shingles of the world.

By now we seem to have come to a sea which has gone out for ever. It is not the same kind of sea as the one described at Dover in the first stanza, but it may strike us that where there 'the eternal note of sadness' was brought by the sound of the waves coming in, here the misery seems to be brought by their going out. And furthermore it may then occur to us that in the second stanza what the poet talked about as miserable-sounding was the movement both in and out, the to and fro motion of the waves. So we seem to have not only shifts of mood, but opposed forms of tide or wave imagery conveying that mood.

But in the last stanza, which is the darkest yet, we do not seem to have any more waves or sea at all:

> Ah, love, let us be true
> To one another! for the world, which seems
> To lie before us like a land of dreams,
> So various, so beautiful, so new,
> Hath really neither joy, nor love, nor light,
> Nor certitude, nor peace, nor help for pain;
> And we are here as on a darkling plain
> Swept with confused alarms of struggle and flight,
> Where ignorant armies clash by night.

Now there is only harsh, darkened land, racked with violence. To some extent we see the poet justifying his change of vision in the poem by saying that the world may look glorious to us but is not so in fact: yet that is not quite the way we have experienced it. And we might at this stage begin asking questions. What makes him become gloomy? Is it any one thing? He says it is the eternal note of sadness; then he says it is 'the turbid ebb and flow/Of human misery', whatever that is; then he says it is not so much eternal as the loss of a particular spiritual strength man used to have; finally he says that joy is a sham and all is simply bleak and miserable. And as we began to see, he keeps changing the images with which he describes these various miseries, from a full sea to a bare land. What sense can we then make of what he is saying? Is it any more than mere shifting mood that governs his statements? They do not seem to stem from any clear or single cause. Further, we might even hit on the question: if there is, as he says in the last stanza, no 'certitude' in life, then how can he be certain of the very things he is saying about it here? If nothing is sure in life, then what surety is there in his vision? And we might, after some thought, go further and even suggest an answer to this very question. The poem shows the poet's moods and images constantly shifting: might that not in fact be an imitation, whether or not intended, of the very fact that there is no certitude in life? He has kept making general statements about existence which are neither justified nor congruous with one another: does not that depict him as a creature as much governed by life's incertitudes as anything else? It is perhaps a too curious speculation, but it is one invited by the poem, and one that leads at least to a stimulating reflection.

We have thus got far enough with observation of the poem's inconsistencies to proceed on our own to try to make sense of them, if sense can be made. This, of course, to put it formally, is done by the method of making 'connections' described in Chapter 5. Actually we have already gone some way towards this. The sea in the first stanza is brim-full, with the tide in. In the next we hear of it going in and out much more. Then we hear of a sea which has gone out for good. Lastly we are on bare land which seems to have known no sea. If we take what the poet says in the last stanza at face value, namely, that what looks good is actually, when considered more deeply, wretched, we might trace a process of increasing 'wretchedness' or bleak awareness through the poem after its initial seeming happiness. In other words we could see the poem as describing a kind of stripping process, whereby happy illusion is steadily pared away for bleak truth.* And then we could make the connection with the sea imagery, which itself is stripped away to bare land. The changing and seemingly

---

* Curiously, though, it is also a movement which goes steadily inwards to the mind, from the objective world of the calm sea at Dover described in the first stanza, through the remembered literary sea of Sophocles in the second and the conceptualised Sea of Faith in the third, to the wholly subjective world of the 'darkling plain' which replaces the sea in the last stanza.

inconsistent sea-images when compared with one another, would become 'consistent' in this larger design or theme of showing a mind actually in the process of stripping its illusions. So we would then be dealing with a situation in which it would be a mistake to look at the poem any longer too locally: it would be wrong to ask how a tide that goes to and fro and a sea that goes out once and for all can be made consistent with one another in producing the same sense of misery, when we are actually dealing with a process in which each generalisation is simply one more temporary stage on the way, and each image the changing record of the stages of that deepening journey.

As suggested, the forms of inconsistency that can be observed in literature are many. And far more than those that are purposeful are those that are not. Such 'unproductive' inconsistencies, if we may so call them, are damaging to the effect of a work. Most generally they can be said to spring from a division of purpose in the writer, which manifests itself by the work going in opposed directions. A striking form of this is the forcing of a work which has in some way rebelled against social norms into a conformist conclusion. George Crabbe's poem *The Village* (1783) starts as an attack on all those, whether ignorant pastoral poets or well-fed and remote farmers, who either idealise or ignore the lot of the rural peasant, which Crabbe proceeds to expose as one of unmitigated misery and exploitation. Worn down by the harsh environment, unceasing labour and poverty, the rustic is shown sinking inevitably to decline and death, speeded by the miseries of the parish poorhouse and unaided either by the doctor or the parish priest who are supposed to help him. So ends Book I of *The Village*, with the perfunctory rites of a pauper funeral: and so we feel, the poem is set fair in its second book to underline what has clearly the makings of a social, even (dangerous in those days) a revolutionary protest. Yet if we expect this of Book II, we are to be disappointed. The Crabbe who indicted the rich and those remote from the rustics in the first book now turns to attack the rural poor themselves as a source of degraded morals, disease and possible insurrection. Preservation of the property of the squire and the bourgeoisie becomes of paramount importance. By the end of this book, Crabbe has gone so far from the rustics that he can devote a lengthy pæan of praise to an aristocrat, one Lord Robert Manners. Manners himself had no connection with the rustics, and indeed at the very moment that Crabbe is using him as a kind of spiritual model he points out how far his condition transcends that of the peasants. Crabbe evades the programme of social change the earlier part of his poem would seem to invite: he silences the rustic clamour which he himself allowed vent by proposing the value of the very social order he earlier seemed to attack; he runs from his own revolutionary instincts to those of a frightened conservatism. And in doing so he forsakes his own best inspiration: the poor texture of the writing in Book II is itself inconsistent with the penetration and bite of that in Book I.

The kind of inconsistency which moves from rebellion or freedom to conformity is often to be observed in literature. Similar to the effect produced in Crabbe's poem is that in Dickens's *Oliver Twist*, where the very social order of middle-class indifference which attacked for the miseries of Oliver in the parish workhouse in the earlier part of the novel, turns out to be the class to which he himself belongs, a class full of worthy philanthropists and dewy-eyed ladies of charity. Simultaneously, Oliver is transported from the scene of institutionalised evil to the clutches of a gang of criminals under Fagin in London: the source and blame for vice is now shifted from society itself to those who live outside it.

Conformism in literature may, however, also work to produce a conclusion which may be more reassuring, wholesome or morally acceptable to the reader or audience than the preceding matter might have augured. Such, we have already suggested, may be the case with Ben Jonson's *Volpone*, where the dramatist clearly struggled to bring about a punishment of the brilliantly depraved Volpone which would be convincing. Such, too, seemed to be partly behind the 'happy' ending where truth was finally accepted in Edward Albee's *Who's Afraid of Virginia Woolf?* The energy of antagonism which the play seemed partly to celebrate was felt to be lost in the flat togetherness of this conclusion. Morally 'good' it might be; morally uplifting in the best American sense to come to terms with the truth about oneself and one's life: but the play is too full of excited images of destruction and violence for this to appear anything more than suburban platitude.

William Golding's *Lord of the Flies* may be considered another form of inconsistent conformism. The background of the story is one in which nuclear war has taken place, and a plane-load of schoolboys is stranded on an island, with the pilot and all adults dead. What Golding traces is the progress towards barbarism in the boys. Whether he intends this barbarism as a commentary on what has happened in the larger adult world is not clear: given the common belief that the child is nearer the primitive than the adult, such a connection may be harder to make. At any rate the boys eventually divide into two camps: Jack, the more violent leader, grows increasingly savage and pits himself with growing support against Ralph, the boy who represents responsibility and trust in the civilised world and its values, and Piggy, the fat boy, who 'represents' the rational, scientific instinct. In the end, Piggy is killed and Ralph is hunted for his life by what is now a savage tribe under Jack. Yet, at the very last moment, just as primitivism seems dominant, Ralph's maddened flight leads him to the beach and to the feet of a naval officer who has just come ashore from a ship. This officer, immaculate in his white uniform, demands to know what is going on and is amazed to find a group of British *children* behaving as they are: '"I should have thought that a pack of British boys . . . would have been able to put up a better show than that"'. At one blow the consequences of human behaviour are annulled, and comforting 'normality' returns: we may have been shown the depths to which unattended children may sink, but we are left with the impression that only children could do this, and that the continuing influence of parents, adults and civilised values would make it impossible anyway. The story is shorn of much of its generalising power, reduced to the level of a freak situation; and the dark vision it presents, of moral and social value steadily lost or destroyed, is cancelled at a stroke.

Observation of such inconsistencies as these is relatively easy compared to the detection of inconsistencies in an argument or process. We simply feel one part of a work to be strikingly at variance with another. Often however, as we have seen, such observation may reduce the strength of a work, and because of this we may be reluctant to pursue it further. This is where the difficulty in these cases comes in: if we are to understand the work truly for ourselves, we must follow our intuitions whenever they take us. We ourselves must be non-conformists.

We can end here with the mention of a few other types of 'inconsistency' that may be encountered. Sometimes a story may be felt to defy its own moral. It is possible to feel with the Middle English poem *Pearl*, where a grieving father is granted a visionary meeting with his dead daughter on the border of heaven, and she with seeming harshness tells him he is an ignorant, earthly fool to grieve over her, that there is a certain frozen character to heaven which makes its dictates less than fully adequate to sorrowing humanity; a humanity for whose sorrow God, as more 'incarnational' Christianity has it, sent Christ as comforter. We may feel with Defoe's *Moll Flanders* that the evident zest with which the various sexual, marital and financial escapades of the heroine Moll are recounted by herself throughout the novel make her protestations that her life is intended as a moral lesson to her readers merely an attempt to be 'respectable'. We might find similar discrepancies between the life and the morality, or worldly and spiritual promptings, in others of Defoe's novels, such as *Robinson Crusoe* or *Roxana*: though with these we may not feel the moral element to be so perfunctory.

Then there are the sorts of inconsistency where we feel a book ends more happily – or more sadly – than it should. We may feel that the evident power of realisation that Tolkien has given to the evil powers in *The Lord of the Rings* makes the victory of the 'good' seem nugatory and manipulated. We may feel that Dorothea Brooke in George Eliot's *Middlemarch* is granted an idealised escape with the romantic Ladislaw from the realities of provincial life, which she has not earned, and which is out of keeping with the entrapments in their own predicaments in which all the other characters are left. We may feel, on the other hand, that the endings of some of Thomas Hardy's novels, such as *The Return of the Native*, *The Mayor of Casterbridge* or *Tess of the d'Urbervilles*, are much more pessimistic than they need be, through the use of coincidences and pieces of extreme bad fortune in the plot to produce a wretched outcome. Any of these feelings can provide a way towards a deeper understanding of a work, whether of how these limitations arose, or, in some cases, of how they are only apparent, and actually emerge from an underlying pattern of coherence we could not otherwise have seen.

We may also find inconsistencies of character behaviour, inconsistencies of texture, of plot, of tone, of style, violations of the laws of the fictional world, inconsistencies between 'intended' and 'achieved' meaning. Shakespeare's *Measure for Measure* can provide an instance of the first two. The rigorously ascetic Isabella of the first two acts, who is a novice nun, is to be found in the middle of the play assisting in a scheme whereby another woman may be seduced in her own place by the rapacious Angelo: she, who detested extramarital sex in her brother Claudio with Juliet and was prepared to let the law take its fatal course with him, now actively brings about such an act to save her own chastity. Such an inconsistency will reflect rather more on Isabella ironically than on the play itself perhaps. But this might not be said of the way that the play can be seen as changing from a dramatic contest and debate over the issue of Claudio's fornication into a mere 'hugger-mugger' of plotting by which to circumvent its consequences: from this point of view, what was a complex interaction of characters and beliefs with a possibly tragic outcome descends to the level of mere manipulation of events to secure a happy ending, during which time the initial identities of the characters are largely lost as they become ciphers.

Beyond this the reader is on his own, and will doubtless have in mind inconsistencies which none of these classifications cover. But the main point should be sufficiently clear: literature is often founded on disjunctions and subject to inconsistencies, some of which may be damaging, some revealing a deeper purpose than we could have known, but all of them, once apprehended and considered, bringing us closer to the life of the works in which they occur.

9
Multiple
Disjunctions

What we will be dealing with here are much more complex forms of disjunction. Here the disjunctions themselves are not only many, but occur in apparent separation from one another within a text; often they all look different from one another; here, if we like, the disjunctions are themselves mutually disjoined. Both seeing the several disjunctions themselves, and then 'connecting' them up into a pattern of sense, involves a special kind of critical energy.

As said, it is not often easy to recognise such chains of disjunction. In the first place there is our natural tendency to ignore discrepancies in a work of literature, to try to wear them down as part of a need to gain a single unified impression, and simply to avoid interruption to our reading. Why carp about little things when there are so many more immediate impressions and effects to be gained from the work? Again, it is going to be a fairly active critical mind that not only notices disjunctions, but compares them to see whether they are all of a kind or not. But our business as literary critics is to get beyond immediate impressions, to notice smaller crosscurrents in a work and to see where they may lead. Nor need observation of small things lead to small conclusions: indeed they can be the hairline traces that show the structure of a work to be quite other than we may have supposed.

Thomas Gray's *Elegy Written in a Country Churchyard* seems at first sight plain enough. The narrator of the poem – who is here 'dramatised', and not to be simply identified with Gray himself – is sitting in a village churchyard near the close of day, watching the country people go home and the darkness gradually close in, and is led to think on the rustic dead all

about him and the sorts of lives they led. He begins by
describing their lost joys and activities: once these were men
who went out gladly every day to work and returned at
evening to the welcome of their families; but now this will
happen no more:

> The breezy call of incense-breathing Morn,
> The swallow twitt'ring from the straw-built shed,
> The cock's shrill clarion, or the echoing horn,
> No more shall rouse them from their lowly bed.
>
> For them no more the blazing hearth shall burn,
> Or busy housewife ply her evening care:
> No children run to lisp their sire's return,
> Or climb his knees the envied kiss to share.
>
> Oft did the harvest to their sickle yield,
> Their furrow oft the stubborn glebe has broke;
> How jocund did they drive their team afield!
> How bowed the woods beneath their sturdy stroke!

In the way the speaker has it, that 'No more' comes to sound
as though all these activities have stopped for everyone, in a
kind of universal end of all things: the morn, the cock and the
swallow will no longer call them up, the fire, the wife and
children will no longer welcome them back. It is an odd way
of putting it, even if it does perhaps heighten the sense of
finality in their loss. If we ask, what is it that the speaker
shows to have been lost, it is not so much the villagers for
themselves, as the links between them and their environment.
We do not hear anything about them personally, only about
how they acted or were acted on by others. These sounds
called them up, these people welcomed them home, they bent
the harvest, ploughed the ground or felled trees. What is lost
is a fabric of connections. Strangely, the speaker does not even
describe the activities of the villagers' lost days in sequence
either; first we get the early morning departure, then the
evening return, and finally what they were doing in between.
   In the next stanza the speaker turns to defend their labours
and lives:

> Let not Ambition mock their useful toil,
> Their homely joys and destiny obscure;
> Nor Grandeur hear with a disdainful smile,
> The short and simple annals of the poor.

On a first reading, this stanza is unlikely to strike us as strange. It seems to be doing what the rest of the poem so far has been doing, lamenting the loss of these poor and humble people and valuing the lives they had. But, when we come to think more about the poem, we may be aware of a slight shift of direction here which in previous readings we perhaps ignored. So far the speaker has simply commemorated the rustics: has told us of the lives and environment they will no longer have. The description of their labours seems a straightforward praise of something good: they brought in the harvest, they ploughed the fields, they cut the trees; and with what amazing vigour! The land seems to have bowed in acknowledgement of their strength, their power over it. There is almost something kingly in their past actions, with the land as a recalcitrant subject brought to heel. But in this next stanza we suddenly find the poet defending their rustic labours, saying they should not be mocked or disdained. We most of us never thought they should: why, we might ask, introduce this defensive note? And curiously the speaker is now talking about their lives as 'homely' and their destiny as 'obscure'. That was not at issue before: the speaker was simply talking about their lives on the assumption that they were worth talking about. There was no critical element, no sense that their lives might be in any way lacking. And it seems a rather odd defence of them that admits that they are 'homely', 'obscure' and 'short and simple' – one that gives reasons for disdain even while it insists that such disdain should not exist. And, we may reflect, what have Ambition and Grandeur got to do with it at all? They were not in the poem before: why suddenly introduce them now?

Some such thoughts may occur to us on thinking hard about this stanza and its details. But just one such oddity is not perhaps going to disturb us overmuch. It is maybe a bit awkward, introducing as it does new issues and areas of concern, but perhaps the speaker is simply trying, if not very successfully, to show that rustic lives can be valued beyond the countryside – that, say, great men should sit up and take notice of the daily lives of country people, which are as important as anything they do. Do not scorn them, he is saying, for they have as much in their way to offer as you in yours. Perhaps we might even begin to speculate that the poem might be taking a 'communist' line, whereby the work of ordinary people is seen to be more real and solid in worth than that of 'great' men: maybe even we consider that the great are described in terms of empty abstractions, 'Ambition', 'Grandeur', as against the very physical and strongly-felt lives of the rustics.

If these are the sort of lines we think along, we are not allowed to rest in this view:

> The boast of heraldry, the pomp of power,
> And all that beauty, all that wealth e'er gave,
> Await alike th'inevitable hour:
> The paths of glory lead but to the grave.

This says that the most powerful, magnificent, beautiful and rich of people come to nothing in the end. What it is also saying is that just as the peasants come to death, so do the great. And still more it is saying, 'Ambition and Grandeur should not mock the lives of rustics, because they like the rustics will die in the end'. So we have to ask: is this the answer to the issue raised in the previous stanza? It certainly is not saying, as we might have supposed, that peasant life and work is as good or valuable as that of great people. In fact it seems to have dropped the issue of life and work altogether. Instead of talking about equality in life, it talks of equality in death, all levelled with the dust. If we were rustics, it would not be much of a consolation to be told that we could be equal with the great in the grave. It certainly would not go far to remove any feelings of neglected worth we might have. So then the speaker's answer here does not seem a very good one. He could easily have argued that the *life* of the grand was of no greater value than that of the rustic, as the last stanza might have led us to expect him to do, but he chose not to, chose rather to give this 'death levels all' answer which hardly meets the issues of the rustic's potentially disdained 'destiny obscure'.

So why did the speaker not produce a satisfactory answer? We can say if we like that he is not presented as a good thinker. We can dismiss the issue altogether and proceed with the poem as a straightforward elegy, as far as we can. Or we can hazard a guess. The whole matter seems to come down to the insertion of Ambition and Grandeur in the first place: why did the speaker bring them into the poem, why did he not just carry on talking about the loss of the rustics, the heavy hand of death that has cut them off from the village and their families? It almost seems as though the speaker has got a 'thing' about rank, as though he cannot talk about peasants without thinking of them as potentially 'low' and looking over his shoulder at the attitude of the 'high'.

Let us now look at several of the succeeding stanzas:

> Nor you ye proud, impute to these the fault,
> If Memory o'er their tomb no trophies raise,
> Where thro' the long-drawn aisle and fretted vault
> The pealing anthem swells the note of praise.

> Can storied urn or animated bust
> Back to its mansion call the fleeting breath?
> Can Honour's voice provoke the silent dust,
> Or Flatt'ry soothe the dull cold ear of death?

> Perhaps in this neglected spot is laid
> Some heart once pregnant with celestial fire;
> Hands, that the rod of empire might have sway'd,
> Or waked to ecstasy the living lyre.

> But Knowledge to their eyes her ample page
> Rich with the spoils of time did ne'er unroll;
> Chill Penury repress'd their noble rage,
> And froze the genial current of the soul.

> Full many a gem of purest ray serene,
> The dark unfathom'd caves of ocean bear:
> Full many a flower is born to blush unseen,
> And waste its sweetness on the desert air.

The general drift of this is still evidently in support of the rustics, and in commemoration of them: those happy to read the poem as straightforward elegy will continue to do so. But is the subject of that elegy the same? Earlier in the poem it was the rustics as rustics. Now, however, the speaker is saying that perhaps some of them had the potential to be great: 'Hands, that the rod of empire might have sway'd'. So we have to admit that he is lamenting the peasants in two opposed modes: first as peasants, and then as peasants who could have been better than peasants. And, if we consider, we can see another difference. Where earlier he mourned them all, here he is saying that we should not disdain them, for some of them might have had great, if stifled, abilities. But that means that only *some* of them might have been potential great poets or rulers. Thus he is no longer lamenting all dead rustics, but only some of them: and this because they could have had the potential to stop being rustics.

Consider the stanzas in more detail. What do we make of the first two? The speaker says, 'Don't, you great people, condemn the poor because they have no grand funeral services or memorials. After all, your monuments and proud inscriptions have no power to pull you back from death'. Does the second stanza really answer the issue raised in the first? The first points out the apparent discrepancy of the memorials and says we must ignore it. The second tries to produce an answer, but the answer produced is not the one needed. To say that wealthy memorials cannot smooth or help to reverse death does not meet the point that prompted the previous stanza, namely that the rich have great tombs and the poor scant memorial. No amount of saying that the one is no more efficacious than the other is going to alter the fact that the real difference is that the rustics are left without much to mark their previous existence in the world, while the great will not readily be forgotten. And here it may begin to occur to us that part of the object of this very poem is to provide just such a monument and an epitaph that the peasants do not otherwise have.

Why talk about the difference of memorials anyway? One can certainly see how the speaker has happened upon it. First he said the great were not to feel contempt for the lives of the rustics; then, to give 'justification' to this, he said that all classes were equal in death in the end; then of course, having mentioned death, it was a natural transition to discuss gravestones. If we read the poem at the surface level, we will unconsciously take in this pattern and accept it without question. At any other level it certainly begs questions. Why, for instance, having denied final difference in life, is the speaker now discussing another side of it in death? It looks as though he cannot leave the subject of class difference alone. And is the speaker really on the side of the rustics? He proceeds in the next three stanzas to say that we ought to value them because they might have possessed the talents we see in the great. But this is to accept the standards of the great as a means of valuing the rustics. They are not to be appreciated any longer for themselves, but only as they might have become great men. And in doing this, the speaker is led to portray the condition of being a rustic as a wretched one: it is that condition which chokes talent, represses noble rage and freezes the genial talent of the soul.

Suppose we were to say, 'Well, all the speaker is really doing throughout is defending the rustics: it is that which makes him try to prove them equal to the great in any way he can, even if that means stressing the talents that could have made them great and no longer rustics'. Certainly one can see how he has tried to prove them equal in death, and then moved on to try to prove them potentially equal in life, and this gives rise to possible inconsistencies. And we might, were this all there was to be said, simply stop there and accept the inconsistencies as minor accompaniments to a generally clear single purpose. But we must still wonder why it was that the speaker first felt it necessary to prove the peasants and their lives and deaths equal to those of the great. He had been getting on quite simply with the business of describing the happy lives the rustics once lived, in a mood of elegiac contrast: why did he then feel he had to defend them against potential censure or mockery? A poem which started as elegy becomes one of evaluation. So we are driven to some such conclusion as the one mentioned earlier, namely, that the speaker feels pulled between the simple life and the life of fulfilled talent among the great. Of course we do not formulate this view at this stage of our reading of the poem: it is done in retrospect, from reconsideration of our impressions as we moved through it.

Reading on then, we pass through the speaker's further portrayal of the kinds of talent that may have remained in embryo among the villagers: there may have been a village-Hampden, a Cromwell, a 'mute inglorious Milton' among them (st.15). They might have received acclaim for their oratory, wielded great power or wealth, or enriched their country (st.16), but this 'their lot forbad' them. Equally, however, they might have been vicious, shameless, or tyrannical (sts17–18). Instead, the speaker says,

> Far from the madding crowd's ignoble strife,
> Their sober wishes never learn'd to stray;
> Along the cool sequester'd vale of life
> They kept the noiseless tenour of their way.

What do we make of this? For is not the speaker effectively saying, 'they lived far from the vain world of the great and they lived happily'? And how does that square with the attempt we have just seen to show that some of the rustics could have had the expression of their talents in the great world had it not been for their wretched lot? Before they were 'repress'd' and 'frozen': how can the speaker see them as soberly and cheerfully choosing the temperance of a lot he has just shown as unavoidably confining and stunting? Again, we can see how he got here: he only wants to defend the rustics, and this has led him into saying they may have had talents equal to those of the great, but these were not expressed through circumstances beyond their control; but since this implies a gloomy view of their repression, he tries to show them accepting it, tries to suggest, quite inconsistently, that they are better off without the crazed world they might otherwise have entered. None of this, however, can remove the basic sense of inconsistency, which stems from the fact that the speaker cannot praise the rustics simply for themselves.

By now enough has been done to stir up the poem, and to offer some tentative explanation for its cross-currents; and we can go on to build up larger interpretations for ourselves. We will not linger over this here, save to suggest some lines of thought arising from what we have seen. The poem starts by describing the severance of the dead villagers from their former lives, with its repeated 'No more'. Then it tries to show that the rustics are not to be scorned by the great, that they might have been great themselves had they not been prevented. Two different subjects seem to be present: that of the dead in relation to life, and of village life as against great life. Again, one can see them as different sides of the poet's own personality, now drawn towards the village, now to the larger world. But still, they are two topics, and are worth comparing. And if we set them side by side and let our minds work on the question of why they are in the same poem and whether there is some deeper connection between them . . . . Well, they are both about divisions and disjunctions, of death from life, and of life from life (or class from class). Both the dead and the living rustics are in their own ways cut off from the world. Seen thus, they are metaphors of one another; and the poem gains an unexpected measure of unity.

Maybe too we could consider further the way the poem keeps changing direction on the subject of rustic worth. Later it is to change direction in another way, by introducing a persona of the poet himself into the landscape. It seems unable to settle to any fixed view or context. It may just occur to us that restlessness is in one way the central topic: even the dead are described as unable to lie in peace (sts22–3); the living are intermittently portrayed as frustrated; and the poet cannot hold any steady view of them. (Even the description of evening calm at the beginning of the poem is disturbed by the 'droning' beetle or the complaint of 'the moping owl'.) The poet we are to meet later in the poem (sts24–32) is also an unquiet figure as he moves unhappily about the landscape. In this light all the different features of the poem come together; and its very disjunctions, disjunctions both of subject and of stance, can be seen as unconsciously serving to mirror the restlessness that is its theme.

And if we are thinking of the whole poem, what is its purpose? What the poet describes here are people who are forgotten: their talents unseen, scorned by the great, lost in the grave, without even adequate epitaph. Suppose, then, as we began to do earlier, we consider this poem itself as an attempt to give the rustics the epitaph and the recognition they have not received? In that sense it would not be a poem merely, it would be an act. We might think along some such lines: and perhaps we might even find ourselves considering that the act of literary criticism itself, the process of making connections, may here be allowed to be more than a purely aesthetic pursuit. But it is enough to suggest such lines. The main business here has been to show how a developing awareness of the disjunctions in a work can lead, when these are connected up, to a transformed sense of the work's characters and meaning. It is not, as said, an easy activity, for it involves not only noticing the disjunctions but tracing a pattern among them, and out of that drawing conclusions and perhaps detecting larger patterns still.

For another example we can consider Shakespeare's *King Lear*, which arguably exhibits a number of shifts in expectations of behaviour – shifts which are therefore different in character from those of apparent attitude in Gray. At first sight there may seem nothing particularly odd about the start to the play. We have a brief scene in which the Duke of Gloucester and the Earl of Kent are talking, with Gloucester's bastard son Edmund also present. They discuss a division of the kingdom intended by the old King Lear: the possible recipients appear to be only the Dukes of Albany and Cornwall, no mention being made here of Lear's married daughters, nor of a third possible beneficiary in Lear's youngest daughter Cordelia. Kent asks to be introduced to Edmund, and Gloucester embarks on a half-apologetic, half-breezy account of Edmund's illegitimacy, to which Kent politely remarks that, 'I cannot wish the fault undone, the issue of it being so proper'. Gloucester proceeds to mention another, and legitimate, son, Edgar, whom he says he loves no more than Edmund. He then asks Edmund if he knows Kent, and introduces him. He tells Kent how Edmund has been away for nine years, and is going to leave again. The scene stops here with the entrance of the King.

There seems little in the scene to surprise us. Gloucester is garrulous and a bit selfish and coarse: he does not introduce Edmund until he wishes to do so, not when Kent asks; he speaks of Edmund as though he were not present; he seems rather crude in his joking about Edmund's bastardy, and perhaps we feel a slight twinge of unease as he says he likes his legitimate son no more than Edmund. Perhaps, were we Elizabethans, we might as they did take the matter of bastardy more seriously: but as things stand, Kent does not, and we are not encouraged to.

Later we find Edmund plotting to discredit Edgar with his father, for his own advancement. He forges a letter from Edgar, inviting him, Edmund, to dispose of Gloucester, and arranges matters so that Gloucester will 'catch' him trying to conceal it, ask for it, and then the more readily believe it to be from Edgar. By keeping Edgar and his father apart, Edmund is able to keep telling each of moves against him by the other, until he arranges a scene where Gloucester will come to seize Edgar, and Edmund and he will be found apparently fighting before Edgar's 'escape'.

What then do we make of the later suffering of Gloucester? In terms of the plot of the play his eyes are put out by Regan and Cornwall because he tried to help their enemy King Lear. But later it becomes clear from the way Gloucester keeps speaking of how 'I stumbled when I saw', that his pain is to be seen as in some sense a fitting punishment for earlier blindness. Now at this stage we either accept this and go on watching – and after all the 'plot' reason for the blinding (the rage of the evil at Gloucester's helping of Lear) is there to mask the moral one – or we may ask whether Gloucester's extreme agony is not in excess of his crimes. And – what crimes? After all, it could seem far more Edmund's fault that Gloucester came to distrust Edgar; and as for his attitude to Edmund, it seems no more than casually vulgar and egocentric. So what do we do? We can if we like settle for the answer in the nature of tragedy. For tragedy, we are often told, does not observe proportion between the sin committed and the pain thereupon experienced: tragedy exists in extremes of disproportionate and largely undeserved pain. This is to take for granted that we know what 'deserving' means, and can measure it. Alternatively, we can be left with what amounts to a sense of outrage at the play itself: it is not fair, we may feel, that Gloucester should have so much pain for something he did not do, no matter how much he claims he did. This level of outrage at least opens up further questions. Was there something more in Gloucester's behaviour than we saw? And if we did not see it, are we not perhaps in some sense as casual and superficial as he is made to suffer for being? Perhaps we should consider what is happening with Gloucester, Edmund and Edgar much more closely. He (Gloucester) listens to the illegitimate son tell an illegitimate story; he puts the false before the true. More than this, he does not *know* either Edgar or Edmund: if he did, he could not have believed the lies of Edmund for a moment. We might think along some such lines, though probably we would not take them so far at this stage. But what is interesting here is that a disjunction in the causal sequence of the play has suggested a reading of the preceding matter at a further level. That level is no longer that of causality or even of psychology: we are forced to a level of symbolic understanding to make coherent connections of desert and consequence.

Suppose we now look at the play from the 'Lear' angle. We first see Lear when he has called his court and his daughters about him to announce that since he is old he is resolved to divide the land among his children. Then he says that the best part will be given to the daughter who can show she loves him most. His first and second daughters Goneril and Regan proceed to make fulsome declarations of their love for Lear. When he turns to his youngest daughter Cordelia, however, Lear finds that she is able to say 'nothing'. She says she cannot 'heave/My heart into my mouth'; then that 'I love your Majesty/According to my bond; no more nor less'. These are two seemingly opposed reasons for her inarticulacy: one, that her love is too great to be spoken; two, that it is not to be talked about, being a natural debt. Pushed by Lear, she says more: that she cannot protest all her love for her father, for if she married she would give half of her love to her husband, leaving only half for her parent. On hearing this, Lear flies into a terrible rage and banishes her.

If we are reading or watching this for the first time it may not occur to us that Lear is being in any sense evil up to the point of his outburst. It seems reasonable enough to give away the kingdom 'that future strife/May be prevented now': if he carried on as king into his dotage, order and control might collapse. That he has to *divide* the kingdom among his children may not seem to bode well, but it is clear that he has at least two powerful factions to appease. So much for the overt politics of the situation. As for the 'love test' itself, it certainly comes as a bit of a jolt, the sudden intrusion of apparently private matters of personal emotion into a public occasion, and it may well seem at least indecent of Lear to have asked for such public statements from his own children. But we have not yet been given any direct hint that Lear is to be criticised, and at this stage we may be quite ready to see the test as a means for Lear of gaining statements of fealty before a large number of witnesses in order to secure the future. At any rate we are likely to feel that it is only fair that he should give the best of the kingdom to the child to whom he thinks he is dearest, since it is in his gift.

All seems just reasonable enough, to the point where Cordelia makes her refusal and Lear breaks out with

> Thy truth, then, be thy dower!
> For, by the sacred radiance of the sun,
> The mysteries of Hecat and the night;
> By all the operation of the orbs
> From whom we do exist and cease to be;
> Here I disclaim all my paternal care,
> Propinquity and property of blood,
> And as a stranger to my heart and me
> Hold thee from this for ever.
>
> (i.i.107–15)

It is a terrible curse, uttered in rage no doubt, but pronounced in chillingly deliberate terms: it involves not only the goodness of the sun but the evil of black magic and the night; it is not simply the disinheriting of a child, it is the annihilating of one. We seem at one stride to have been taken into another dimension altogether. Or have we? Is the Lear we see now so sheerly different from the Lear we saw before? It is at this stage that we begin to look back to reconsider our earlier view of Lear's behaviour. The apparent disjunction, the jolt we feel leads us to ask whether we have understood only superficially till now. Soon Kent is to say to Lear, 'See better': he might perhaps be speaking to us too.

What too of Cordelia? Could it not be said that she rather provokes this rage by the bluntness of her refusal to her father? One usually expects the third child in a fairy tale to be the kindest, but here, in a rather fairy-tale situation, she is effectively being the cruellest. Here his best loved daughter is telling Lear in prim terms that the best she can offer him is 50 per cent of her love. Surely if she really loved him she could humour him, let him down gently? And it is not necessarily true that she cannot love him 'all' because of the love she might have for a husband: it is possible to love both one's parent and one's husband or wife with all one's heart; possible to say that love is not less for being divided. Curiously, she seems to be using the very notion of division of love that Lear is trying to apply as a yardstick for the apportioning of the kingdom. Could she not have said to Lear, 'I do love you, but I cannot talk about it or measure it in words, for love is not that sort of thing'? Instead she first says this to herself ('I am sure my love's/More ponderous than my tongue'), and then talks in quite different terms to Lear.

If we think along these lines, Cordelia becomes in some way blameworthy: we look at her as a fallible human being. We think of her as a prig, or as someone who cannot resist putting the moral knife in, or as a cold person, or as a jealous sister furious that Lear should attend to the others before her. All of which readings are rather unfortunate in the scene, since she is effectively portrayed as the heroine who sees the falsity about her and is prepared to reject all worldly advantage for the truth. As Lear casts her off, Kent tries to dissuade him and to show him that there may be more truth in Cordelia's plainness than in the hyperbolic statements of their love for Lear by Goneril and Regan. Lear says, 'Let pride, which she calls plainness, marry her': but, as the scene proceeds, we see that Cordelia really is plain and not proud. Why then, to ask the question again, did she have to speak so?

These are small matters, doubtless. Then let us look at some of the large ones. If Lear was only a silly old man making a single error of judgement in that first scene, he is certainly made to pay dearly for it in the play. His daughters strip him of his followers, cast him out on a wild heath where he goes mad; though he meets Cordelia again, it is only to lose her when she is murdered, and then to lose life himself as he looks on her. As with Gloucester, we seem to have an enormous discrepancy between the size of the act done and of the suffering experienced as a result of it. And as with Gloucester, we will be forced back to that opening scene to consider its implications more deeply, to ask ourselves whether there is not more there than we thought to make Lear in part at least deserving of what he is to suffer.

And the same reinterpretation will be needed with Cordelia. If we have continued to see her at the level of a jealous or cold young woman, we are going to feel something of a jolt when we find her become almost a symbol of pure love later in the play. Lear, run mad, knows only that the road back to sanity is through Cordelia and asking her forgiveness. Cordelia comes back to Britain to help him, sends out men to find him and bring him to her for healing. She is portrayed to Kent, hearing of her father's miseries, as the lady of sorrows, full of sympathetic love and compassion, not enraged but profoundly grieved by the actions of Regan and Goneril.

> 'Sisters! sisters! Shame of ladies! Sisters!
> Kent! father! sisters! What i' th' storm? i' th' night?
> Let pity not be believ'd!' There she shook
> The holy water from her heavenly eyes,
> And clamour moisten'd; then away she started
> To deal with grief alone.
>
> (IV.iii.27–32)

This saintly view of her is going to be hard to reconcile with any previous view of her as in any way irritable, jealous or priggish that we may have derived from the last time we saw her, in the opening scene. (And actually we hardly see her at all in the play, which makes our initial impression all the more important.) We are forced therefore to ask ourselves whether our initial impression of her behaviour may have been inadequate, and whether here again we must 'see better'. Perhaps, for example, her earlier manner of speech in rejecting the 'love test' arose not out of jealousy but simply out of integrity, a refusal to fudge the issue and allow any refuge in sentiment. Given her reported passionate feelings for Lear here, however, that again may seem a little hard to accept.

Maybe, then, we should not be seeing her earlier behaviour in personal terms at all. We always, we could say, try to bring saints down to our own level, attribute to them our own seedy motives: doubtless in this often thin mortal air their voices can sound more bleak and cold than they really are. Perhaps then it is the medium that is responsible: there Cordelia is placed, in a context in which she is asked to pervert the truth and make a sole god of a man – notice how we are now

entirely reinterpreting that opening scene – a father so ignorant
of the natures of his own daughters that he not only has to
make them declare their love for him but is able to believe
the empty protestations that Goneril and Regan make. If we
make this sort of reappraisal, it, of course, involves us as
audience in reappraisal of our own superficiality, and hence
makes the play much more morally effective. In this sense we
will be saying that the disjunction is 'meant' to be there, to
drive us back to knowledge of how much we too are implicated
in the very evils the play attacks.

By now we have noticed several apparent disjunctions in
the play: that between what Gloucester seems to be and the
pain he has to endure; that, similarly, with Lear; and that
between the earlier and the later Cordelia. At some stage,
probably earlier than this, we will have begun to put the
situations of Gloucester and Lear together, and we can observe
that in each case the situation involves a division between
parents and children, or, putting it more narrowly, between
male parents and their good children, with only the words of
the bad children believed. There is some sort of pattern of
divisions in the play: and indeed if we look closely we will
find the word 'division' itself cropping up frequently. And
perhaps here other discrepancies in the behaviour of some of
the characters in the play may come to mind. (It is of course
quite wrong to suggest that this is the sole order in which we
think about the play: we could have noticed other disjunctions
long before the ones we have discussed, or have come to quite
different conclusions from the ones presented here.) For
instance, is not the behaviour of Edgar a little odd? Is it not
strange how ready he is to believe what Edmund says about
his father Gloucester's belief that he (Edgar) has been plotting
against him? Would one not expect him at least to try to find
out the truth of this for himself? Still more, would one not
expect him to try to meet Gloucester and account for himself?
Instead, he agrees to be concealed by Edmund, the very
person who is plotting against him; thus by his absence no
doubt adding to the cloud of suspicion put over him. Still
more, when Edmund has Gloucester come upon Edgar in his
house, he 'warns' Edgar of his father's approach, and then
has him engage in an apparent fight with him (Edmund),
before making off; whereupon Edmund can cut himself on the

arm, and pretend to Gloucester when he enters that Edgar
gave him the gash in a violent struggle which ensued when
he (Edmund) refused to agree to the murder of his father.
The point, of course, so far as Edgar is concerned, is that he
believes that Edmund is trying to pacify Gloucester on his
behalf and accepts that Edmund will be compromised in his
father's eyes if he is found to have harboured Edgar willingly:
but really none of this 'plot' element can get round the
strangeness of the situation in which the father and the son
are so consistently separated and on such flimsy motivation.
We have to ask too, if we blame Gloucester for listening to
the false son rather than the true, where does that leave Edgar
and his readiness to trust the word of Edmund against his
father?

At this stage we might, using the method of comparison,
put the behaviour of Edgar and Cordelia together, since they
are both good children spurned. Each is supposed by the
father to be bad: each seems at first sight curiously inert or
inept when under paternal question. This similarity further
weakens local psychological readings of this behaviour: there
is something more general as its cause. In both cases the
father listens to the false, and the true either cannot speak or
sounds harsh . . . . Could we not begin to argue that the
goodness of Cordelia and Edgar simply cannot come through
at this point in the play because evil is the dominant
power? In this case their behaviour will become, as it were,
metaphysically governed. The fact that Cordelia, Kent and
Edgar are banished, and that the last two can only exist near
Lear or Gloucester in disguise, whether as the servant Caius,
or Poor Tom the beggar, would then also fit into this: since
goodness is not recognised by Lear and Gloucester, it must
go hidden until they change. This very reading would explain
why the disguised Edgar does not reveal himself to the ruined
Gloucester he leads about for so long in the play until the
latter is near his end – another apparent disjunction, pointed
to even by Edgar himself when he blames himself for his 'fault'
in not disclosing himself before. For if it is a case not of Edgar
disguising himself but of Gloucester being for long unable to
recognise him; if the repulsive disguise is an emblem of the
dimness of moral vision in this play, then it is not Edgar who
uncases, but Gloucester who at last sees him for what he is;

not psychological, and hence voluntary, reasons, but spiritual ones, prolong the disguise.

We are ready now to bring together other disjunctions we may have noticed in the play. Minor, perhaps, is Kent's rather coarse treatment of Goneril's servant Oswald. Oswald has not done anything overtly unpleasant to Kent (as Caius) at all, yet we find Kent tripping him up before the king in Goneril's house, and later setting about him when they meet as messengers to Regan from Lear and Goneril respectively at Cornwall's castle. Kent when asked says that his ultimate reason for attacking Oswald was that 'His countenance likes me not': he hit him because he simply did not like the look of him. Cornwall finds that hard to take: and initially we may too. But we may consider that such an answer removes local causes: it is not for what he has done, but what he is, that Oswald is loathed. Insistently Kent directs our attention to the essential rather than the accidental. Always we are asked to go beneath the surface, and the seeming disjunctions of the play help to push us in this direction. Why does Edgar choose, of all disguises, that of a mad beggar? He thereby makes himself a singularly appropriate figure for Lear to encounter after he has begun to realise his folly and see something of the pride from which it issued. But more than this – which in itself suggests the 'spiritual' rather than psychological cause behind the disguise – Edgar's disguise can be seen as symbolic of the beggary, the outcast, unaccommodated condition, to which goodness and truth have been reduced in this play. Cordelia has been banished dowerless, Edgar disinherited: these two themselves symbolise that reduction of goodness. Perhaps we even notice here how much the play uses the word 'nothing': everything must be reduced to nothing in this play before it can become anything.

We may find other and larger disjunctions too. Are Goneril and Regan really so bad? Does Lear not provoke them by battening on them with what is evidently a very unruly crowd of 100 knights while still keeping to himself the name of king? It would be quite an imposition for anyone . . . . And yet we are to believe them primally evil for trying to restrain Lear, and for eventually being forced into a position where it looks as though they thrust Lear out at night when he chose to go himself. And is it not a bit of a jump to find two sisters with a reasonable grievance against a demanding parent suddenly turning into two savages actively engaged in hunting down and killing Lear, or in gleefully assisting in pulling Gloucester's eyes out? And, on another tack, is it not a trifle hard to accept, as many of the commenting characters would have us do, that Lear's one night out in the wet was as prodigious a piece of suffering as that of Gloucester being blinded? Looked at as we have been doing, these questions are not so much asked by us as thrown at us by the play. It says, 'Here you feel the discrepancies: find yourselves answers if you can, see through to the truth if you are able, and learn it if you dare'.

Here we have found, as with Gray's *Elegy*, that where disjunction is a recurrent feature in a work, it is usually also in some sense the subject of the work. *Lear* is about disjunctions: not only apparent ones, which we must see through, but real ones, which last. For we can make all the connections we like, but we will still be unable to overcome the disjunction essential to tragedy, and one felt most poignantly in this play, the gap between the initial bad act and the enormous evil, suffering and waste that come of it. At this point we can begin to ask about the 'world-view' behind *Lear* – is it pessimistic, stoic, just? Gloucester sees the cosmos as arbitrarily malignant: 'As flies to wanton boys are we to th' gods – /They kill us for their sport'. Then Kent finds life chaotically determined, 'It is the stars, /The stars above us, govern our conditions'. Albany tries to claim that the universe is one in which the good and the evil alike find fitting reward, 'All friends shall taste/The wages of their virtue, and all foes/The cup of their deservings'. None is right, yet all of them have a piece of the truth, because no single world view is adequate to encompass what happens in *Lear*, and there is a radical disjunction between any one view proposed and the hard facts. *Lear* is not wholly meaningless, as the evil do meet their fitting end; and yet it is 'meaningless', in that Cordelia dies. Ripeness is not all, for whatever ripeness is gained is largely forfeit in sudden death. Human choice no less than fate governs the conditions of the characters in the play. Whatever unitary meaning we or the characters try to draw from the play it at once swallows and rejects. It is an ordered chaos, a mixture of such meaning with no meaning that we are at once drawn to make sense of it and refused that sense even as we think we have gained it.

There is one last question we might leave ourselves with: does Lear really develop into a true spiritual awareness over the play? How much is real, how much is what we want to be there and put there to give coherence to his experience? Suppose we have to accept that he does develop, but not into the saint that we would have him? Suppose we were to ask how much he comes to a sense of the wrong in himself rather than in other people?

It may now occur to us at this point, with the analysis taken thus far, that there is a central image of disjunction in the play. It is Dover Cliff. The blind Gloucester is led by the disguised Edgar to Dover, where he wishes to kill himself by throwing himself from the cliff. Edgar takes him to a place which he says is the very edge of the cliff, and goes into detailed description of the enormous gulf yawning below. Actually it is not the cliff edge at all. But Gloucester believes him, and throws himself 'down', to be met at the 'bottom' by Edgar in another guise, telling him of the enormous height he has fallen, and yet how he floated down like a feather. Still then Gloucester believes he did fall down the cliff, and that fate has preserved him. The cliff, as we said, is a symbol of disjunction, a vast abrupt in the ground, as in our understandings as we read the play. But in fact there was no cliff at all. What seemed a gulf, seen more clearly, is no gulf at all. Equally, what seemed discrepancies in characters' behaviour or consequential experience in the play proved on closer analysis to be not finally discrepant at all. Yet even that is too simple, for there is a cliff, and the cliff is described in vivid, if imaginary, detail in the play. There both is and is not a cliff, just as there are and are not disjunctions in the characters' behaviour or in the actions of the play or in the visions of the universe it presents.

If we find a text which produces a sense of numerous disjunctions of this sort, then however much we have to analyse our experience to find them, they can when put together and considered produce a new insight into the work. Sometimes multiple disjunctions are built into a genre, or are otherwise easy to spot, as in mock-heroic, or in conceited poetry which uses far-fetched metaphors; but often we are only going to notice them by having our sensibility at a 'high resolution' setting. Particularly the mind has to be free of flattening preconceptions, whether they be that such disjunctions are to be ignored as trivial, or that no great work admits any apparent gap in texture, or that we must let what we assume to be the broad subject or direction of the work obliterate our sense of its often manifold counter-elements. This is the cast of mind required for the activities and procedures described in most of the chapters of this book.

10
Structure

A way into a text may often be found by considering its structure. This involves asking why the parts of it are in the order they are, why it begins with one item and not with another, and why the string of items that makes it up occurs in just this sequence and no other. When we ask this question we can often find a deeper pattern not only of organisation but of meaning in the work than we might otherwise have seen; and certainly we often find an unsuspected road into hitherto perhaps resistant material.

There are circumstances in which we will be less inclined to ask such questions of structure. A straight narrative of causality, such as a detective story, a romance of developing love, a narrative of action towards a fixed objective, may not invite questions of its organisation, since each event forms an evident chain leading towards an end, and where such connections are already present we are not so strongly impelled to look for others. This is not to say that such works do not contain other forms of bonding determining their order: a novel may contain a plain narrative and yet at the same time have a larger pattern, as Patrick White's *The Tree of Man* follows something of the mythic pattern of the Book of Genesis even while it is supremely realistic. But we will most immediately be stimulated to investigating matters of structure where a text appears in some way to call for it by being apparently unstructured or unconsequential, or else by drawing attention to its own symbolic content or other strangenesses of juxtaposition within it. There is also something else that can operate as a determinant in attempts to find the hidden principles behind a work, and that is quite simply its fame: if it is celebrated by general opinion, and yet appears to us at first sight banal, flat or limited in range, we are tempted to find out what else may lie behind it.

Consider Swift's 'A Description of the Morning':

> Now hardly here and there an hackney-coach
> Appearing, showed the ruddy morn's approach.
> Now Betty from her master's bed had flown,
> And softly stole to discompose her own.
> The slipshod prentice from his master's door
> Had pared the dirt, and sprinkled round the floor.
> Now Moll had whirled her mop with dext'rous airs,
> Prepared to scrub the entry and the stairs.
> The youth with broomy stumps began to trace
> The kennel-edge, where wheels had worn the place.
> The smallcoal-man was heard with cadence deep,
> Till drowned in shriller notes of chimney-sweep.
> Duns at his Lordship's gate began to meet,
> And Brickdust Moll had screamed through half a street.
> The turnkey now his flock returning sees,
> Duly let out a-nights to steal for fees.
> The watchful bailiffs take their silent stands,
> And schoolboys lag with satchels in their hands.

This is a very vivid account of an early eighteenth-century street. We can almost see the coaches beginning to steal along the bare streets in the chill dawn, or the more proximate Moll whirling her mop, almost be at the shoulder of the youth hunting in the gutter for old nails, or hear the different morning cries, followed by the strange silent congregating of the duns and bailiffs, and the limp, straggling progress, everlasting down all time, of the reluctant schoolboys. Many readers would be, and have proved to be, more than satisfied with so clear-eyed a postcard from Augustan London. Why ask for more when we have what is so plainly an inside view of a moment in time that brings times together, and for a brief instant seems to obliterate our sense of alienation and distance from history? It cannot be denied that this has value, even if it is not directly literary value.

Yet the way that the whole is presented as a bare limp list, united only by the fact that one item seems to come naturally after another, prompts speculation as to whether there may not be some principle of organisation behind these snapshots which makes it fair to call this a poem rather than a series of random views. Is there any way that we can say that the whole piece has some kind of internal unity, some patterning behind the sequence of its details? The most important thing almost is to get as far as this question. The yield we get from trying to answer it may or may not be worthwhile, but without it there may be no yield at all. So let us put the poem again before us and then analyse what feelings we have. The first thing that may strike us is the verbs. They begin in the past tense: 'Now hardly here and there an hackney-coach / Appearing, showed the ruddy morn's approach'. Much of the rest of the poem is in the past or the pluperfect tense: Betty 'had flown', the prentice 'had pared the dirt', Moll 'had whirled her mop', the youth 'began to trace', the 'smallcoal-man was heard', 'Duns . . . began to meet'. But in the last four lines the poem shifts into the present: 'The turnkey . . . sees', the bailiffs 'take their silent stands', the schoolboys 'lag'. Can we make anything of this? Perhaps Swift just blundered into it. But still we can ask ourselves how appropriate such a shift of tense might be in the poem. If we consider that it is a poem about waking up, we may be able to see some significance in the change to the present. We could see such a change as imitating the way we come fully to ourselves. When we are awake we are, pun notwithstanding, fully present, at one with reality once more. That is how it feels, too: we feel a sudden extra brightening and vividness as we come to those present tenses.

And this can throw light on the previous past tenses too. It is not too great a jump to shift from the equation of present tense with being close to reality to seeing the past tense as mirroring being out of it. And in this connection we will find it particularly striking that the time is so frequently 'out of joint', as it were, in the early descriptions. We must feel something of a jar with those 'Nows' alternating with pluperfect verbs. Certainly the 'Now' at the beginning of the poem, especially when followed by the present participle 'Appearing' which starts the second line, leads us to expect a present tense verb; and when we get the past 'showed', the jolt is considerable. And so it is with 'Now . . . had flown', and 'Now Moll had whirled'. This again is heightened when at the end of the poem 'now' goes, as we normally expect it to, with the present tense: 'The turnkey now . . . sees'. The very use of the pluperfect tense gives and as it were takes away an action. To tell us that the prentice *had* pared the dirt from the door puts us at some undefined time afterwards. If Swift had said, 'Now Moll has whirl'd her mop with dext'rous airs, / Prepared to scrub the entry and the stairs', we might feel close to her about to do the scrubbing: but the pluperfect throws us further off. So all this dislocation through tenses would fit with the sudden sense of some 'location' through the present tense that appears in the last four lines.

The poem is yielding some structure: and not only formal structure, but one that is related to what it describes. But still, this seems only a little to go on. Are there other features in the poem that show patterns? If we consider carefully, we may see that the poem moves on the whole from indoors outwards. It is true that we start with the coaches entering the streets. But then we are set in the inner sanctum of the house, 'master's bed'. Betty, in leaving it for her own room, begins, as it were, to open the doors of the day. But still we are inside. Then, we find, we move to the slipshod prentice paring the dirt from around the outside of the door; then further on to Moll at the foot of the stairs preparing to scrub the entry and the stairs; and thence to the youth outside tracing the gutter. The smallcoal-man's and chimney-sweep's cries that are heard seem to be heard from where we now vaguely feel ourselves to be, on the edge of the street outside the house in which we began. But then the poem seems to venture further: we see the duns at 'his Lordship's gate', we are halfway down the street with Brickdust Moll, we see the turnkey, the bailiffs and the lagging schoolboys at some further indeterminate place. We have moved from indoors progressively outwards to a steadily more inhabited street. We can say, if we like, that this too imitates a process of waking up and going out, just as the change of verbs brought us finally to ourselves. We can go further and conceptualise it: this pattern accomplishes through change of place what was earlier seen to be also done through change of time.

By this point we can, given practice, perhaps see another and parallel shift present in the poem, one from singulars to plurals. The people early on are on their own: Betty, indeed, has just separated from her master. The prentice works alone,

Moll has to get on by herself with her work, the youth tracing the kennel is solitary. But then the smallcoal-man *'was heard'*, implying a relationship; and he does not cry alone, for his voice is drowned in the shriller notes of the chimney-sweep. We may just notice also that previously each isolated individual took up the two lines of a couplet, while now the couplets are shared by two different individuals each with one line. What before was 'The slipshod prentice from his master's door / Had pared the dirt, and sprinkled round the floor', is now 'Duns at his Lordship's gate began to meet, / And Brickdust Moll had screamed through half a street'. Further, the individuals are often incongruous with one another – duns and Brickdust Moll, bailiffs and schoolboys, which heightens the sense of plurality. By the end of the poem the previously solitary turnkey is seeing his flock return, duns are meeting, bailiffs taking their stands, schoolboys lagging. All has become much more multiple and various, again in keeping with the increasing activity of the day as it 'comes to itself'.

If we have got this far, however, it may occur to us that the poem does not end on a particularly lively or active note consonant with the day's beginning. Instead of being left with movement, we are left with a rather odd freezing of motion: 'The watchful bailiffs take their silent stands, / And schoolboys lag with satchels in their hands'. The bailiffs are ominous, waiting only to dispossess someone of his goods; the schoolboys, however typically, do not greet the day with any of the exuberance of youth. If we consider the feel of that couplet, we may be struck too by its bleak finality. Each line seems heavy, as though driven in. If we look back at the rest of the poem, we may perhaps see where this feeling comes from. Most of the preceding couplets ran the sense of the first line over into the second. The coaches are appearing, Betty leaving her master's bed for her own, the prentice paring the dirt, Moll preparing to sweep the stairs, the turnkey waiting for his flock, each over two lines. Even the smallcoal-man exists over a couplet, as his cry is drowned by that of the chimney-sweep. In two cases the syntax itself goes over the two lines: we have to wait for the second line to understand fully what is being said with the coaches and the prentice. But in these last two lines of the poem each item is radically divided from the other, confined to its line. We may then notice that the change is partly in the syntax too. 'The watchful bailiffs take their silent stands' is a straight subject-verb-object statement, and the account of the schoolboys is similar. Other couplets often have inserted prepositional or adjectival phrases between subject and object: 'Now Betty from her master's bed had flown', 'The slipshod prentice from his master's door / Had pared'. 'The youth with broomy stumps began to trace': there is none of the hard definition of those last lines. Perhaps it arises too from the hard rhyme of 'stands/hands', harder than any previous rhyme sound in the poem. It is also a matter of the statements being in parallel: the bailiffs wait, the school-boys lag; both oppose motion. No other couplet has quite this parallelism of meaning and form. The voice of the smallcoal-man is interactive with that of the sweep. The duns who meet at his Lordship's gate are different from Brickdust Moll who, in a much more sprawling line, 'had screamed through half a street': they draw in, she gives out; the account of them folds them in with a verb, where Moll's verb 'screamed' throws its way down the succeeding 'half a street'. As for how far the sense of the preceding poem has prepared us for this rather motionless ending, we may, if we look back, see some change in the way actions are described. At the beginning of the poem they really occur, while towards the end they are only in prospect or frustrated. The coaches appear, Betty goes back to her own bed, the prentice pares the dirt. Moll, however, is only preparing to scrub the stairs, and the youth is only beginning to trace the kennel-edge. The smallcoal-man's voice is lost. Duns begin to meet, they do not act. The turnkey's flock comes back to prison. Brickdust Moll has screamed through only half a street.

No doubt there is more to be gleaned from the poem. But we have got to a point where the patterns we have traced mirror two different movements. The changes from past to present, from indoors to outside and from single to more multiple figures, suggest the increasing life of the day as morning comes. Yet at the same time the heavy, static feel and meaning of the last lines, the way they work against previous fluencies and mixings within the preceding couplets, the way too they are also a culmination of a pattern of increasingly frustrated action in the poem, work against any cheerfully vitalistic reading: the poem ends in some inertia and foreboding. Beyond this we can say what we will: can say if we like that Swift has played with our cheerful assumptions about day to show that there is another side. But the important thing for us is to have seen the patterns, to have found that what seemed a mere straightforward list can actually be found to have a great variety of hidden patterns that add to its suggestiveness and power of implication. And that is what the determination of structure can often do, and often with the most unpromising of material.

There are several forms which the determination of structure can take. The one we have just looked at involves taking a simple list of items and finding a developing pattern within it. The structure of a work may equally imitate a dominating idea or image in it (no such idea was evidently present in Swift's 'Description'). Wordsworth intended in *The Prelude* to recapture the growing effect of nature upon him, and it is not surprising therefore to find the form itself of the poem, with its frequent changes of direction and sequence, coming over with all the abruptness of nature itself, or, to be more specific in one instance at least, of a winding river (described as being like the poem at the beginning of Book IX). The central image of Dickens's *Bleak House* could be said to be a house itself: at the beginning of the novel the characters are all divided and seemingly disconnected from one another, like a heap of bricks, and it is by means both of inquiry and the connectiveness of charity that in the end all is discovered, the house of fiction stands complete, and a new Bleak House is built. The 'structural' image of the mandala in Milton's *Paradise Lost* we have already seen. In Coleridge's *The Ancient Mariner* the journey of the mariner through different landscapes can be seen as images of the development of his soul. The fact that H. G. Wells's *The Time Machine* gives progressively less space to the further travels of the Time Traveller towards the frozen end of the world beneath a dying sun could be said to be imitative of the process of entropy described. The architectural or painterly analogy frequently used by eighteenth-century literary critics to characterise the works of their day, or the musical analogies used by the Romantics, may serve as structural principles behind their work.

It would be hard to cover the many forms that structure itself can take. Sometimes it can be extremely formal, as when Renaissance poems use certain numbers of lines or stanzas in their work to symbolise ideas; or when poems are written so that their shape on the page imitates their theme, as in George Herbert's 'Easter Wings'. But there are some structural patterns that are fairly frequently to be found in literature. One might be called 'Hegelian', in that it moves from thesis to antithesis to synthesis. Andrew Marvell's 'To his Coy Mistress' starts by saying that if the lovers had all the time they wanted, the lady's coy delay could last as long as it liked; but then the poet-lover says that this is not so, and our lives are short; he therefore proposes that they overcome any passivity, long or short, to time by living their lives so fully that they will transcend it, and though they cannot make the sun 'Stand still, yet we will make him run'. The novel *Jane Eyre* shows the heroine moving from the sensual Rochester to the equally (though differently) appealing ascetic St John Rivers, and finally back to a Rochester who has lost some of his passion and gained moral insight: the two drives in Jane's life, the passionate and the spiritual, are at last fused in the one man. The pattern of elegy too, frequently follows the course of recall of a lost life of value, contemplation of the wretched world that remains, and then a consolation that lies through and beyond the pain: thus for example Milton's *Lycidas*, Shelley's *Adonais*, or Auden's 'In Memory of W. B. Yeats'. Another structure is the evolutionary one, where each item is reflective of some developing condition within the work, as in almost any account of spiritual change, from Langland's *Piers Plowman* to Conrad's *Lord Jim*. Circularity too can sometimes be found as a structural principle in literature. Wordsworth's *The Prelude* ends at the point in Wordsworth's development where he will be able to write the poem that has just described it: for Wordsworth all our life must be an attempt to rediscover our beginnings. Shakespearean comedy, as in *A Midsummer Night's Dream* or *The Winter's Tale*, has a circular form in returning to the place where it began. So too does much modern fantasy. Another form of structure is that of paired opposites, as in Milton's poems 'L'Allegro' and 'Il Penseroso', Blake's *Songs of Innocence* and *Of Experience*, or in the vision of D. H. Lawrence's *Women in Love*. We shall look at one structural use of (balanced) opposites a little later. Commonest of all is the kind of series we have just examined, where apparently discrete items have hidden links that turn them into a chain. A variety of this is the series which narrows or expands, each detail either being 'larger' or 'smaller' than the one before. Pope's *The Dunciad*, starting from single Dunces and gradually increasing the numbers until all forms of dullness that ever were have been covered, is one kind; as (differently) is Kingsley's *The Water-Babies* where Tom's journeys take him to wider and wider expanses of water mirroring the development of his soul. Equally Sterne's *Tristram Shandy* could be said to be founded on a structural principle of diminution, whereby much is made of increasingly less.

As an instance of the expanding series we can consider in detail Edmund Spenser's *The Faerie Queene*, the long Renaissance poem portraying chivalric behaviour under several heads of virtue. Here as with the Swift poem, though for different reasons, the text appears at first sight antagonistic to any 'structural' reading; and this will serve to heighten the applicability of the method. In his long introductory letter to the poem (written before the publication of the first three books), Spenser avowed that his objective was to write a poem of altogether twenty-four books, twelve celebrating the private virtues and twelve the public, according to an Aristotelian scheme, and all aimed at fashioning 'a gentleman or noble person in vertuous and gentle discipline'. In fact, the poem as it exists has just six books and a little over two cantos of a seventh. The virtues treated in these books are Holiness, Temperance, Love, Friendship, Justice, Courtesy, and in the seventh, entitled *Two Cantos of Mutabilitie*, Constancy, which last is not so much a human virtue as the principle that allows the universe to exist. Now it is open to us simply to say that the poem is unfinished and to leave it at that. But it is also possible for us to consider whether even with its fragmentary aspect the poem may have a hidden structure. Such a structure, if discovered, could be explained in terms of a gap between Spenser's conscious intention for the poem and his unconscious achievement. If we do look for a structure, however, it must as with all criticism be one that arises naturally and convincingly from the material: there must be no intellectual game-playing to force into being what is not substantially there.

Suppose then we do. It is clear that we cannot find a single theme running through all the books: the knightly contests may be similar, but the virtues are different, and are only to be corralled under one head by eroding their separate identities: they all go to make up the ideal man of Magnificence, portrayed in the introductory letter as the summation of all twenty-four virtues, but each does not represent one twenty-fourth of that magnificence, for that only comes into being when they are all present. Of course there is Arthur, the ideal, who enters in the eighth canto of most books to put right the difficulties encountered by the knights of that book, and he is Magnificence, but he only demonstrates that every virtue is present in Magnificence, not how magnificent is the individual, and often on its own fallible, virtue of a Guyon, a Britomart or an Artegall. But we can look at this another way. Arthur is the achieved gentleman the poem seeks to fashion: he is the end point of the twenty-four books, yet is there from the first. The poem thus has an aspect of having got where it is going before it goes there – and to this extent the number of books completed is not important. So now from trying to see the poem in unifying and thereby reductive terms, we can look at it as a sequence.

The interpretation that follows here is, again, only an instance of what can, with practice and reasonably lengthy acquaintance with the poem, be done; it is certainly not intended as the sole truth. It could just strike us, though, if we let our minds play over the whole poem, that the series of virtues it deals with grows progressively wider in scope, moves from individuals outwards. For if we consider Spenser's letter in which he said the first twelve books were to be about private virtues and then the next twelve were to be on public or 'politicke' virtues, the six or so that we have do not appear to agree. The first book, on Holiness, deals with a virtue which we could fairly call a private, or at least a personal one. The concern of the book is not centrally with the dissemination of the Christian faith, nor with the Church as an institution (though it can be partially allegorised in these terms): its focus is on the way in which the individual deals with evil promptings that emerge from within the self, even if they come also from a supernatural source – with pride, loss of faith, despair, the impulse to blaspheme. And the same is true of the second book, on Temperance: the battleground is the soul of the knight Guyon, and the whole is symbolised in the image of the human body, the Castle of Alma (Cantos IX–XI). And in a sense this is of the essence of these virtues. Holiness does not exist between two people: it may be observed by one in another and so cause benefit, but that is not the same thing. And the same is true of Temperance. But in the third book of *The Faerie Queene* the virtue treated is Love: and this necessarily involves other people for its existence. And in the fourth? – Friendship, into which, just as the characters and actions of the third book overlap into the fourth, Love shades.

By now we are dealing with virtues that are increasingly 'public': by now too we are beginning to look for a pattern of gradually widening reference in the poem, from the personal outwards. Love involves just two people. Friendship can take in more: Book IV we find deals with larger groups of people than Book III. In Book V the virtue is Justice, and here we move out to relationships within society as a whole, the bonds that keep men in harmony: throughout the book the concern is frequently with whole groups of people, from the ignorant multitude who follow the falsehoods of the 'communistic' giant, to the trains of Munera or Radigund and the nations of Belge and Bourbon. Thus seen, *The Faerie Queene* as it is contains political virtues originally intended for later books. In Book VI the concern is also with society and conduct therein – Courtesy, which might be said to balance with Justice. And in the seventh book, we find, we deal with universal relations, the principle that binds all things. Mutability claims that change is the universal condition and demands chief place in the cosmos, but Nature replies that change is only the mode in which things become more fully themselves:

> I well consider all that ye have sayd,
> And find that all things stedfastnes doe hate
> And changed be: yet being rightly wayd
> They are not changed from their first estate;
> But by their change their being doe dilate:
> And turning to themselves at length againe,
> Doe worke their own perfection so by fate:
> Then over them Change doth not rule and raigne;

But they raigne over change, and doe their states
maintaine.

(Canto VII, st. 58)

In other words change subserves perfection and therefore
cannot claim universal authority. But, so far as the universe
is concerned, change is the means by which that which is
changeless manifests itself: and here the two great opposites,
of change and fixity, come together. The last move of the
poem, in the two stanzas of the unfinished eighth *Canto of
Mutabilitie*, is to look beyond all this to the largest being of
all, the being from whom all other beings, from the macrocosm
of the spheres to the microcosm of the individual soul,
take their origin. Thus looked at, the poem moves steadily
outwards, into larger and larger contexts, and this sequence
at once structures it and makes it comprehensive in its coverage
of every sphere of existence. The six or so books we have can
thus be seen to do in little the work of the projected twenty-four.

In a sense it could be said that Swift's 'Description',
appearing to be a mere list of items, and Spenser's apparently
incomplete *Fairie Queene invite* consideration of hidden structure: are we to settle for them merely as they appear, or not?
But, of course, formal structure can be found in many works,
even where consideration of it does not seem to be invited.
An instance is the 'Earthsea trilogy' by the American fantasy
and science-fiction writer Ursula Le Guin. The three books
in the trilogy at first seem to contain quite separate stories,
and therefore to form a trilogy only in the loosest sense that
they all to some extent concern the same world of Earthsea
and the same central figure. In the first, *A Wizard of Earthsea*
(1968), a young wizard called Ged releases into Earthsea
through vanity at his own power a formless and nameless
shadow from the realm of evil: he spends the rest of the story
being first hunted by it wherever he goes, and then resolving
to turn and face it, when it in turn flees. In the end the two
meet on a strange land in the midst of the uncharted ocean,
and when Ged names the shadow with his own name, the two
join. In the next book, *The Tombs of Atuan* (1972), Ged rescues
from the labyrinth of the 'Nameless Ones' on the island of
Atuan a young priestess Arha who has been confined there to
minister to the evil gods. In *The Farthest Shore* (1973), something

is draining all the life and magic out of Earthsea, and Ged, now chief wizard in Earthsea, sets out to discover it: he eventually locates it on the far north-western island of Selidor in a wizard called Cob, who is using magic to prevent his own natural death; this wizard Ged overthrows, and the balance between life and death is once more established in the world.

These three stories could simply be taken as a series of adventures showing the growing power and knowledge of Ged in wizardry, together with the moral theme of the humility he must learn and use as a 'mage'. But maybe it occurs to us, whether from the stories alone or from basic ideas within the stories, that there may be a pattern behind them. We are not least helped towards such thoughts by the fact that the idea of secret patterns behind and within the world is one that is basic to Earthsea. At any rate, thinking along these lines, and setting all three narratives together, we may notice that while the first and third involve journeys by Ged all over Earthsea in quest of something, in the second or middle book, *The Tombs of Atuan*, almost all the action takes place in one spot, within the labyrinth of the Nameless Ones. To put it more schematically, there seems clearly to be a pattern, with the middle book at a still point, and the other two mobile about it. And if we think further, we may see that the direction followed by Ged in *A Wizard of Earthsea* is ultimately down the east side of Earthsea to the south-east ocean, whereas that in *The Farthest Shore* is up the west side of that world towards the island of Selidor in the north-west. (There are maps provided on which to follow these journeys.) Put those two movements together, and clearly they are in opposite directions: put them together with the second book as the centre, and we have a movement 'down', followed by a stillness, followed by a movement 'up'. In other words, we see a certain hidden symmetry or balance.

We have reached this insight simply by asking why the three items occur in the sequence that they do. But insofar as the insight is a valid one, we will generally find much else within the work to give hints and nudge us towards seeing it. In this case the plain fact is that in these books the idea of a balance that has to be preserved in the world of Earthsea, is a central and oft-repeated one. We learn in *A Wizard of Earthsea* that the whole world is in delicate equilibrium, an equilibrium which is shaken by Ged's rash act. We are constantly made aware that the job of the wizards who graduate from their school on the island of Roke is to preserve the balance throughout the world of Earthsea, a balance suggested in the very name 'Earthsea' itself. Or as Ged later puts it,

> 'On every act the balance of the whole depends. The winds and seas, the powers of water and earth and light, all that these do, and all that the beasts and green things do, is well done, and rightly done. All these act within the Equilibrium. From the hurricane and the great whale's sounding to the fall of a dry leaf and the gnat's flight, all they do is done within the balance of the whole. But we, in so far as we have power over the world and over one another, we must *learn* to do what the leaf and the whale and the wind do of their own nature. We must learn to keep the balance'. (*The Farthest Shore*, ch. 4)

If we are thus given so strong an idea of balance, or, as it is also frequently called, 'Equilibrium', this is clearly going to be a great help in considering questions of structure: we will simply ask how far the theme is reflected in the form of any one of the novels on its own, or in their sequence as a group. However we work, whether from 'structural' insights back to find a corresponding theme, or in this reverse direction, we are going here to find a remarkable marriage of the meaning and the shape of the works.

Thus fortified with our insights so far into the Earthsea books, we may be ready to look for more. Could not something more be made of the fact that Ged goes to the south-east in *A Wizard of Earthsea* and to the north-west in *The Farthest Shore*? If we follow his journeys on the maps, we find that in the first book he starts in an island in the north called Gont, then travels south to Roke, and thereafter to the west, to the north, to the east back to Gont, and then south all the way along the east side of Earthsea. In *The Farthest Shore* Ged goes from Roke south-east to Hort Town on the island of Wathort, then south, then west right across to the West Reach, then north to Selidor. If we compare these journeys, they not only end going in different directions, but we can see that they also form something like reverse figures on the map. The figure in *A Wizard of Earthsea* is in the rough shape of a 9; that in *The Farthest Shore* is in the reverse shape of a 9, a 6. If we know anything of eastern mysticism, we could see that fitting the two together on the map, to make a 69, amounts to a depiction of the 'Yin–Yang' symbol of psychic wholeness: and actually much commentary on the trilogy has concerned itself with the links between Le Guin's vision and that of the Tao, or of Zen Bhuddism.

However, if we have got this far, we can be more amateur but no less productive for our own purposes. If we see that the one is a 9 and the other is the form of a 6, the next thing to do is to ask us what difference between the stories would fit with this. There are many references we can find to the figure 9 in both books. There are nine lore-masters on Roke, nine months from the time that Ged leaves Roke after bringing the shadow into the world until he finally defeats it, nine stars in the great constellation of Agnen, the rune of ending, which governs *The Farthest Shore*. Nine we may know is a magic figure: certainly Tolkien uses it as such in *The Lord of the Rings*. The motif of the books here seems to be magic itself. But the contrasts: where are they? We can see, for instance, that while Ged is a young man in the first book, he is older in the last. Indeed, we might go on, age itself seems to be much more central in the last book, where we have the old wizard Cob who refuses to die. And what about Ged there? He uses up all his power in defeating Cob and restoring the balance of the world. He returns from Selidor no longer grand wizard, or archmage, but a mere man. And then he goes home to Gont, from where he began long ago. And then it may occur to us, with this circular notion in mind, that in the first book he developed from mere man to wizard: he proceeded in the 'reverse' direction from that in the last book. Therefore the 9 and 6 could be seen as mirroring opposite processes. Beyond this, it might just occur to us that the number nine is associated with wizardry and with the making of magic. The witches in Shakespeare's *Macbeth* say, 'Thrice to thine, and thrice to mine, / And thrice again, to make up nine. / Peace! The charm's wound up' (I.iii.35–7). Under the figure 9 of his journey in the first book, Ged is, as it were, 'wound up' into wizardry; in the last book, under the opposite figure, he is wound down to man. And perhaps more easily we will notice, since at this stage we are looking for any clue that fits in with the idea we already have, that the first book ends in the east, the region of sunrise, and the last in the west and sunset.

This actually is only some of what we might do with these books. We might for example find a highly formal and balanced structure within one book on its own – in *A Wizard of Earthsea*. We might find symbolic reasons for *The Tombs of Atuan* describing what it does, a place of coming together, imaged in the uniting therein of the two longlost halves of a great ring, the Ring of Erreth-Akbe. We might find further reason for the books being in the sequence that they are. Certainly, once 'structural' features begin to show themselves like this, there is doubtless more to be found, and we are certainly in a good position to do the discovering. But the main issue, once one has resolved to try to find a pattern or structure in a work, is simple: always ask why things appear in the order that they do and in no other; and supplement this where relevant by taking a main theme, image or motif of the work and asking how far and in what ways the form of the whole reflects it. After that, the same prescription prevails as in all the chapters of this book: persistent hard thought, constant testing of ideas, practice. When it works, it is not through our ideas being imposed on the material, but as though the text simply yielded patterns that had always been there.

11
Reticence

Try what we may, there is always going to be a way in which
the work we think about finally evades thought and remains
alone, planetary. It is that very alone-ness which in a sense
stimulates the mind to try to possess it in the first place. There
are thus both necessary and obligatory limits to the act of
interpretation. (One current understanding of this is the
notion of textual 'indeterminacy' used by the French theorist
Derrida.)

Take as example an analysis of Melville's *Billy Budd*. The
story concerns the press-ganging of the primally innocent
sailor Billy Budd aboard a British warship, the *Bellipotent*, in
the Napoleonic Wars. It describes the growing motiveless
hatred of the *Bellipotent*'s master-at-arms Claggart for him,
resulting eventually in a confrontation where Claggart falsely
accuses Billy of mutiny to his face before the captain, Vere;
and where Billy, who has a stammer, is unable from outraged
innocence to answer in any way except by a blow so violent
that it kills Claggart and brings about his own summary trial
and execution at sea. The story is punctuated by oblique
comparisons of Claggart, in the peculiarly spontaneous nature
of his hatred for Billy, to Satan in Eden; of Billy to Adam,
although his stammer is portrayed as the blemish of a fallen
condition, and though he is also likened in his innocence to
animals; and of Captain Vere, however criticised, to a divine
father figure, or as Abraham to Isaac with Billy. The way is
thus open for allegorical readings of the story as a critical
reworking of the myth of the Fall and subsequent human
punishment; or with Billy as Christ dying for men at the
behest of Vere as God and trumped-up necessity. We need
not follow this particular avenue, as it is clear from critical
debate about the story that while this kind of interpretation

beckons, it does not fully satisfy. We can demonstrate the need for critical reticence from another approach.

Suppose we review the various details of the story. Billy is a creature of nature, like an animal; Claggart's evil, we are told, is 'Natural Depravity: a depravity according to nature' (chs 2, 11); Vere is seen as a highly civilised man, surrounded and imbued by books, not fully a sailor (chs 6, 7). The narrative is set on the sea, in a ship: the sea is a natural element, the ship is a man-made thing that defies it and shuts it out. Nature and civilisation: we seem to have two terms, and we start checking other details of the story against them. We find that while Claggart's evil is 'of nature', he himself is able to use the forms of civilisation for his own ends: not only that, 'civilisation, especially if of the austerer sort, is auspicious to it [natural evil]. It folds itself in the mantle of respectability' (ch. 11). And then suddenly we may see 'the point' of Billy's stutter. He cannot use the forms of civilisation: when challenged by Claggart he cannot speak, except by uncivilised means (his violence). Then, because this 'natural' act must appear mutiny, however innocent the motive, Vere has Billy hung as an example.

Perhaps at this point we think to the wider context of the whole story, in which the danger of insurrection in the fleet after recent mutinies at Spithead and the Nore is an ever-present threat. Those mutinies, too, could be seen in a sense as the rebellion of nature against civilisation, at least of human feeling against harsh constraint, energy against a too-rigid order. . . . What then of the French Revolution itself, and the revolutionary forces against which England is fighting? Are they not also a kind of mutiny, an assertion of natural rights against the tyranny of civilised despotism? Then possibly we think further, to Vere and the English as Augustans, eighteenth-century men of reason with fixed ideas opposing the incoherent ferment of Romantic energies. And with 'fixed ideas' in mind, we will think again of the sea itself, and how that is a fluid and mobile element, and how Vere and civilisation are pictured as set against it: Vere, we find, has 'a mind resolute to surmount difficulties even if against primitive instincts strong as the wind and the sea' (ch. 22); he sees the forces of revolution as a roaring flood tide, and his own 'settled convictions . . . as a dike against those invading

waters of novel opinion' (ch. 7); he insists that as officers of
the king he and his naval peers are set against nature and
every natural instinct that comes into conflict with the purposes
of civilisation (ch. 22). Then, too, we think that the boat from
which Billy was press-ganged on to the *Bellipotent* was called
The Rights of Man, of which Billy took innocent but ironic
farewell when leaving.

The whole story is by now beginning to be seen in the light
of this motif of nature versus civilisation. Yet what can we
make of it? Clearly we will be seeing the execution of Billy by
Vere as some kind of indictment of civilisation. But why these
circumstances, and these characters? Vere is not a typical
sailor (ch. 7): he is described as not 'fully salted', like, say,
Nelson, which would precisely convey his opposition to the
sea. His brother officers, aware like him of Billy's innocence,
would, we are told, have waited for a fairer trial on board the
flagship of the fleet rather than have convened a summary
'drumhead' court on the *Bellipotent* as Vere has done: they
have in them that which answers to natural feeling. Vere
recognises this natural feeling but refuses it, just as on land
he stood out against the novel opinions 'which carried away
as in a torrent no few minds in those days' (ch. 7). Yet at the
same time, Vere is a man of culture and sophistication, whose
convictions are no mere instinctual prejudice, but the results
of long thought and reading both wide and profound; a man,
too, who feels immense compassion for Billy and pain at what
he feels bound to do to him. If we equate Vere with
'civilisation', then he is civilisation at its finest. In Billy he
meets all that is finest in nature: Billy is the opposite pole of
excellence from himself. Each then is a representative, made
so by the extremism of his characterisation. It is not just that
civilisation is shown as corrupt in what it does: it is that in
the last resort all that is good in civilisation is not good
enough. For Vere, we find, '"forms, measured forms, are
everything"' (ch. 28): the story can be seen not just as the
trial of Billy Budd, but as the trial of civilisation itself, which
in the last resort as here shows itself determined to maintain
those forms even at the cost of outraging the very notions of
justice on which the fabric of civility is supposedly erected.

But if we have got this far, with civilisation thus indicted,
other facts give us pause. For the story by no means comes

down simply on the side of 'nature', or even to any implied prescription of greater response to natural instincts on the part of civilised men. The nature that produced Billy produced Claggart; the nature that in a glorious sunrise gave a Billy whose body, hung from the yard-arm, 'ascending took the full rose of the dawn', also gave those harsh sea birds that swooped at Billy's corpse as it was shot overboard into the deep (chs 26, 28). The tale cannot be recommending a greater acceptance of the instinctual or natural on the part of civilised man when the instinctual is seen as potentially as diabolic as angelic. Claggart, to say the least, complicates the issue. And it is not easy to see a way round the obstacle that he and the other factors here present. Certainly we can cling to the fact of some sort of indictment of civilisation: that does seem to be going on. And yet ... if nature can produce such figures as a Claggart, is civilisation not right to guard against it? The only way out here is to say that it all depends on the circumstances, and that what is wrong with Vere is that he is inflexible. But this forfeits a fair amount of the meaning of the work as we have derived it.

Thus our interpretation takes us so far and no further. It feels 'right'; many aspects of the story answer to it in a striking and unforced manner; and it serves to explain the peculiarly extreme, semi-allegorical characterisation and situation: yet it will not give us more than 70 per cent at most of what *Billy Budd* may be about, before it comes up against the hard wall of obstreperous and contrary fact. And this is often our experience in analysing literature: we look at the data, start with a hunch, find item after item of the work falling in with it, formulate a view of the total meaning – and then find the things that will not fit, however hard we try. Criticism does not generally admit to its own limitations: we will look far to find an article or a book that concedes that its interpretations are partially countered by other elements in the work or works it has examined, but limitations there very often are.

Another recalcitrant element in this story is its style. At first this may seem no problem. If we see Melville as criticising Vere and his devotion to form, it will come as no surprise to find him equally rejecting artistic form, if on the grounds rather of truth than of this theme: 'The symmetry of form attainable in pure fiction cannot so readily be achieved in a narration essentially having less to do with fable than with fact. Truth uncompromisingly told will always have its ragged edges. . . .' (ch. 29). And the frequently digressive character of the story seems to fit with this. The narrative itself comes in brief snatches interspersed with dissertations on 'sailor-cynosures', natural depravity, the character of Vere, the essential irony of naval chaplains on warships, the old crewman the 'Dansker', or the nature of justice. Such a formlessness of narrative might seem to imitate a rejection of form at a thematic level. But while this might be acceptable on the general plane, the detailed character of the style is extremely individual, and gives impressions that go against this interpret-ation. For instance, when describing 'the enigma' of Claggart's hatred of Billy as arising from no specific past incident, Melville tells us that

> the cause necessarily to be assumed as the sole one assignable is in its very realism as much charged with that prime element of Radcliffian romance, the mysterious, as any that the ingenuity of the author of *The Mysteries of Udolpho* could devise. For what can more partake of the mysterious than an antipathy spontaneous and profound such as is evoked in certain exceptional mortals by the mere aspect of some other mortal, however harmless he may be, if not called forth by this very harmlessness itself? (ch. 11)

This style seems nothing if not civilised: its lengthy, complex sentences, its latinate and orotund diction, its citation of a literary work known to few among its readership, its rhetorical questioning, and more generally, its interest in metaphysics, all show a sophistication, a concern with rhetorical forms and definitions which is quite at variance with the 'anti-civilisation' theme we have so far traced in *Billy Budd*. How can an author speak in the very language of a Captain Vere if he seeks to condemn him? How can he speak in such a conscious and ratiocinative manner if the very theme of his story asks the abandonment of such cold consciousness?

There is a way out, but it involves one in half-truths, and in a measure of what might be called critical game-playing. Suppose we say that the above passage simply wastes words: it is saying that Claggart's malignity is motiveless, but it conveys this by an extremely roundabout and repetitive route. What is more, its tortuous nature leaves us relatively uncertain as to what it has been saying. And the same could be said of many passages in the story, indeed of the digressions themselves: their 'object' seems almost to be to lose us. For another instance,

> Long ago an honest scholar, my senior, said to me in reference to one who like himself is now no more, a man so unimpeachably respectable that against him nothing was ever openly said though among the few something was whispered, 'Yes, X – is a nut not to be cracked by the tap of a lady's fan. You are aware that I . . . .'   (ch. 11)

The 'long ago', 'my senior' and 'one who like himself is now no more' are quite irrelevant information, the purpose of which seems only to tangle the thread of discourse to the point where 'a man so unimpeachably respectable' seems for a moment to refer to the honest scholar, since the other person has so far been mentioned only as 'one'. The definiteness of 'nothing was ever openly said' blurs into 'though among the few something was whispered'; the notion of cracking a nut with a fan, let alone a lady's fan, is confusing; and by the time the direct speech is opened, we have so lost the scholar that we take the utterance as that of 'the few' until jerked short by the 'you' and 'I'.

What is the effect of such a style? It seems so reasonable, so urbane, so knowing and respectable (all the things that Vere is and Claggart can feign to be): and yet its effect is to leave us with no knowledge at all, only with an impression of confusion and incapacity to speak directly. It is at this point that we can attempt to link Melville's style to his 'uncivil' theme. The style, let us say, appeals to the 'civilised' man in the reader, and yet it totally frustrates the expectations of good sense and clarity which its assured tone awakens. It implies illumination, yet leaves us with obscurity. But maybe Melville meant to do this. Maybe the style is Melville's way of stuttering like Billy. Maybe in his attack on the 'forms' of civilisation that Vere upholds, Melville has gone so far as to destroy those 'forms' in his own style, here by subverting meaning and showing words themselves as helpless. Maybe Melville encourages the ratiocinative, conscious, civilised side of the reader to respond to his narrative, precisely in order to frustrate and traduce that side by continually pulling the carpet from under it.

Perhaps. We know as we say these things that they sound at once like *aperçus* and rather strained guesses. There is no reason why the game should not be played out to the end, as long as somewhere it is remembered and even acknowledged that it is a game. It is when it is taken seriously, when often tenuous interpretations are seen as the truth about a work, that the danger starts. Danger, because the work itself then loses its life. If it can be caught in a grid of interpretation, if that grid is taken for what it is, then all one has is a dead scheme of meaning. No work of value can be fully described or encompassed by any one interpretation. To be true to what it is, it must be left its freedom at the same time as it is 'caught'. It is not so much that humility is a virtue in itself; it is that it is an aid to accuracy.

This is not to deny that some works are more accessible to ready interpretation than others. One can readily see George Eliot's *Middlemarch* as the portrayal of different kinds of human egoism and blindness, or T.S. Eliot's 'The Love Song of J. Alfred Prufrock' as the portrait of a man in flight from the reality he feels himself called to face. But while these interpretations have truth, they are only the end-point of a process of comparison and analysis: there is still the baffling, mysterious life of the work behind them, a life which will always stand, by virtue of *being* life, in ironic tension with the meanings we draw from it. And sometimes, of course, the mystery comes forward more, whether in the enigmatic *Turn of the Screw* of Henry James, which questions interpretations themselves, or in the unfinished works which we argue are in fact complete, or in the simple mystery of plain irreducible fact.

Take as a last example the following:

> Little piggy
> In the street;
> Motor car,
> Sausage meat.

The tone seems sardonic: the little piggy may appear pathetic, but is reduced to sausage meat. There are no verbs. This gives a sense of inevitability, almost of arithmetic:

pig + street + car = sausage meat; the different objects follow
one another in fixed progression, like a tableau. Yet this sense
of inevitability is played against an equal sense of contingency:
this pig did not have to be in the street, it only chanced to be
there, it is not the typical condition of pigs to be knocked
down by motor cars. But then we may think that all little
piggies end as sausage meat: the first and last lines describe
what always happens; had it not been a motor car that
knocked him down it would have been a bolt in an abattoir.
The contingency of the motor car thus fits back into the
inevitable pattern from life to slaughter, from pig to the
reductive sausage meat. Thus seen, the life and energy of the
poem come in part from this ironic interplay of fate and
chance. Then there is the awful marriage of the terms 'little
piggy' (adjective plus noun) with 'motor car' and 'sausage
meat': they all seem bound into one corporate unit, as though
they could none of them make any sense or have any function
on their own; little piggies are to be killed, motor cars are for
killing them, sausage meat, the product, is almost identified
by parallelism with the motor car next to it. The poem is
almost as bare as it can be, and this increases the bleakness
of its humour. The only concession it makes to direct represen-
tation is in the rhyme in the second and last lines, which may
imitate the squeal of pig and brakes alike. There are other
points that can be made: the 'little piggy' of the first line is
set against three manufactured objects, one of which is the
pig reconstituted – street, car and sausage meat. The pig
perhaps escaped from a van. But what the poem portrays is
that it is always going to be man who kills it: even when it
escapes it is only to another death-factory administered by
man on the road. Indeed, the street and car are almost credited
with turning the pig into sausage meat then and there.

Now all this may say something about the poem, and others
might produce their own different views of what it does and
how it works: but still, in the end, we are left with the sheer
fact of the poem itself, and the potency of the image which its
very brevity conjures up. There are no descriptions of the
street or the car, no verbs describing the movements: we are
drawn to fill them in. And as we do, our imagination is a little
on fire with the creature, loose from its van or pen, running
and squealing about the road until with the rush of a car, all

the more rushing for its movement being omitted, the pig is reduced to a hideous thing and the thing to something we eat, with the suggestion that we devour bodies we have murdered. And these particularisations, which have been urged by the very spareness of the text, in turn are mocked into nonentity once more by that spareness. It is this interaction, this mobility, which is the life of the poem, yet by talking about it one still leaves it somehow separate, untouched. There is the same kind of creative tension between the poem as picture of pig, and the poem as a symbol of the human condition: it is clear that the symbol will not fit man save in some very general way, yet the density of the poem, the sense of 'much in little', drives us outwards to some such feeling which, as soon as stated coldly, will be wrong.

And this is true, more or less, of all literature. The work stimulates analysis; analysis searches, finds, and in finding knows it has not found. To be most true, therefore, criticism needs a built-in reticence. Perhaps this is best to be found by turning it into a game, whereby the interpretations are offered lightly, in a mode of finding without keeping, of seriousness without gravity, of lightness without flippancy. The hardest thing of all, when we have our own original insight into a work, is to admit its inadequacy and even to renounce it. But that is what must happen: once form an interpretation, and our next object is to show its limits, even, to maintain life, to move away from it into another view. Unless we do that, we lose touch with the life and variety that is in the literature.

12
Conclusion

No claim is made that the methods of literary analysis outlined in this book are instantly applicable. The object has been to show them at work, and the ways by which they can help and direct the movements of the mind. But of themselves they will not directly yield results: only practice will do that. And that practice, as often said here, is hard and frequently frustrating work, involving a constant checking of the mind as much as the attempt to drive it forward to a new understanding of the material before it. We have, as much as we can, to stop our personal likes and dislikes for authors getting in our way. We have to learn where the questions we are asking are irrelevant, or where we are concentrating on the wrong area of a text. And many other things. Nor will the techniques described here always provide an answer: quite frequently criticism may require methods of understanding different from those described here, methods involving scholarly or historical knowledge, for example. Nor is it at all possible to show the whole range of contexts in which a given method of analysis may be employed: we have seen here in each case some three examples which attempt to give a spread of different situations in which one might, say, look for 'connections' or make comparisons; but it is impossible to be comprehensive, because every situation is individual.

These reservations apart, it can be said that with due training and close acquaintance with texts, the application of these analytic methods can yield considerable results, and can often produce new approaches to literature. The process is one which, as said in the Introduction, works only through our integration with the text, seeing it and feeling it from within until we know which particular critical switch to throw. It will often be a case of throwing several switches. The technique of close analysis is one that can be productive with a great many texts, and of itself may highlight other techniques we should use, suggesting connections, structuring or disjunctions. And often we will find we are using several of the techniques to see a text in different lights. We might do a close analysis of Wordsworth's *Prelude*, for example, to consider his style; then try to work out the structure of the poem through its thirteen books; compare it with the work of another author; and trace and try to account for its disjunctions. And even within one area, even the analysis of one passage, we may be using two or more of the methods described here. But this is for the reader to explore. Work though it is, the application of these methods can lead to a new sense of the life and energy that is to be found in literature. Indeed, one can be fairly sure that where such life is not being found, where what one is doing makes a text seem greyer, blurred or less interesting, we are doing things in the wrong way. The whole object of this book has been to put some of the life and pleasure back into criticism that it somehow often lacks. What else is literature but the attempts of gifted men and women to give us the best and most honest that the human spirit and their craft can provide? We must try to match their energy or we will never do them justice.

Bibliography

Those interested in seeing extended versions of some of the analyses described in this book may wish to look at my *Literature and Reality, 1600–1800* (Macmillan, London, and St Martin's Press, New York, 1978); *The Gap in Shakespeare: The Motif of Division from* Richard II *to* The Tempest (Vision Press, London, and Barnes and Noble, Totowa, New Jersey, 1981); *The Impulse of Fantasy Literature* (Macmillan, London, and Kent State University Press, Ohio, 1983), ch. 3 (on Ursula Le Guin); and 'Change in *The Rape of the Lock*', *Durham University Journal*, 76, 1 (Dec. 1983).

Index